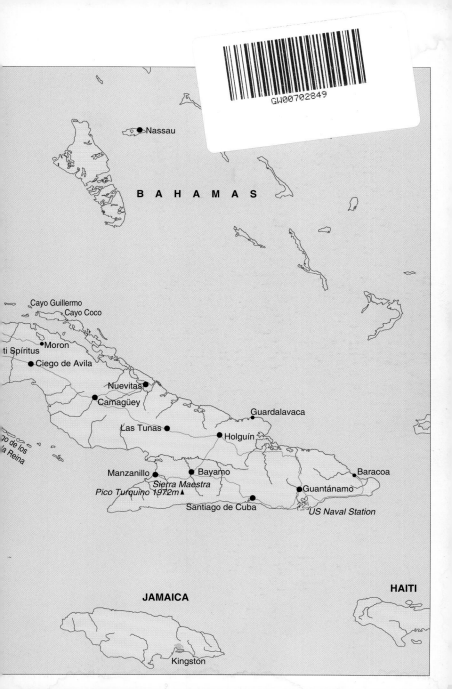

Cuba

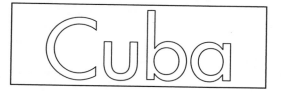

Stephen Townshend

Little Hills Press

© Stephen John Townshend, May 1996

© Photographs Stephen John Townshend, 1996

© Maps by Mapgraphics, Brisbane.

Cover by NB Designs

Printed in Singapore

ISBN 1 86315 102 8

Little Hills Press Pty Ltd
37-43 Alexander Street
Crows Nest NSW 2065
Australia

Moorland Publishing Company Ltd
Moor Farm Road
Airfield Estate, Ashbourne
Derbyshire DE6 1HD
England

(ISBN 0 86190 648 9 - UK only)

DISCLAIMER
While all care has been taken by the publisher and author to ensure that the information is accurate and up to date, the publisher does not take responsibility for the information published herein. The recommendations are those of the author and as things get better or worse, places close down and others open, some elements in the book may be inaccurate when you get there. Please write and tell us about it so we can update in subsequent editions.

Little Hills and are trademarks of Little Hills Press Pty Ltd.

Facing Title Page: Statue of José Martí, Havana.
Facing Page 96: Children in Havana.
Facing Page 97: Dining Al Fresco in Cuba.
Back Cover: National Flag of Cuba.
Inside Back Cover: Ché Guevara.

LITTLE HILLS PRESS
is a member of

CONTENTS

ACKNOWLEDGEMENTS

I am especially grateful to David Collins and Katie Cody for their unselfishly energetic and generous efforts in the shaping and reshaping of this guidebook, and their general guidance which proved invaluable. Much thanks also to Little Hills Press, for early and ongoing support, to Dorothy Button, Barry Carr and Rob Flynn for sharing their formidable professional expertise, and to my Cuban friends Ivan Pedroso and Ernesto Smith, for always having at hand whatever information was needed at a moment's notice.

INTRODUCTION

Cuba is only a small island, yet its international importance has been enormous. Formerly a jumping off point for Spanish expeditions to the New World, then a near protectorate of the USA, and until the late 1980s, a Caribbean satellite of the Soviet-led socialist bloc, Cuba has suffered and soared in its relations with foreign countries.

During the last decade, it has lurched from one crisis to another: experiencing the loss of preferential trade agreements; labouring under the messianic leadership of Fidel Castro; witnessing the daring escapes of *balseros* (boat people) to the US mainland; and waiting out a punishing trade embargo. As a result, Cuba's pulchritudinous cities have teetered and peeled, and scarcities continue to affect consumption and services.

However, all has not been lost. Since the Revolution, Cuba has closed the gap between wealth and poverty, achieved a literacy rate of more than 95%, and guaranteed mass education for its people. In addition, the country's years of struggle have fashioned an experimental and innovative character, and brought some semblance of confidence to a long-isolated people.

Before 1959, few other countries could rival Cuba as a tourist attraction. But when Castro's guerillas seized power, most travellers sought diversions elsewhere. In 1990, lacking a socialist benefactor and deeply in hock, Cuba tentatively began opening its doors to overseas investors. Tourism was targeted as a principal money-maker and it is now the fastest growing sector of the economy and the second largest earner of foreign exchange.

And who can argue with the Cuban government's push to promote tourism? A visit to Old Havana will reveal why Havana was once considered the 'boulevard of the New World and one of the gayest and most picturesque ports on the shores of equinoctial America'. There are grand plazas, shady colonnades, colonial facades, Moorish mosaics and intricate iron-laced balconies, many of which have been restored since the United Nations Educational, Scientific and Cultural Organisation (UNESCO) declared the area a World Heritage Site. You can escape the heat of the day by gracing any number of cafés, and listen as Cubans spiritedly defend their country or talk wistfully of escape.

Outside Havana the countryside of the tobacco and sugar regions of the Pinar del Río Province combine lush hills and valleys full of banana groves and Royal Palms; the southern city of Trinidad, with its

Republic of Cuba

Population: 11 million (51% Mulatto, 37% European, 11% Black, 1% Chinese & Asian)
Capital: Havana (population 2.2 million)
Head of State: Dr Fidel Castro Cruz
Ruling Party: Cuban Communist Party (PCC)
Official Language: Spanish
Religion: 47% Catholic, 4% Protestant, 2% Afro-American Spiritist, 47% Other
Currency: Peso
Exchange Rate: 30 pesos = $US1 (black market)
GDP: 20.3 billion
GDP per head: US$1880
Main Industries: Sugar, minerals, fishing, tobacco, textiles, chemicals
Time: USA Eastern Standard Time

balustered windows, stained-glass arches and cobble-stoned streets is considered one of the best preserved Spanish cities in the Americas; the rugged Sierra Maestra mountains dominate the 'Hero City' of Santiago de Cuba, the most Caribbean of Cuban cities and the 'cradle of the Revolution'; and Varadero, once the playground of US millionaires, is claimed to have the most beautiful strip of beaches in the Western Hemisphere, renowned for their dive sites, underwater caverns and rare sponge coral.

If that's not enough, tempt yourself to an aromatic Monte Cristo cigar, sip *mojitos* at Hemingway's favourite bars, dance the rumba at Havana's famed *Tropicana* nightspot, or frequent one of the many church-cum-clubs where Cubans practice *Santería*, a music-fuelled fusion of African beliefs and Catholicism. You could even find yourself caught up in the dazzling spectacle of Cuba's carnivals, with their kaleidoscope of costumes, masks, decorations, floats, revelry and dancing.

Over 500 years of history has resulted in a country rich in culture, teeming with architectural and historical monuments, and populated by a people who retain an exuberance and hospitality which makes a mockery of their prolonged hardships. And regardless of where one stands on the 'Cuban question', there is no doubting that it is a country that will long occupy a space in the global imagination.

The Amerindians

The earliest known inhabitants of Cuba were the pre-ceramic *Guanahabateys* from Mexico and the *Ciboney* from southern North America. Carbon dating of midden piles and crude tools suggests that they arrived at least 3500BC. Both tribes were cave-dwelling hunter-gatherers and fisherpeople, living in small family groups and

History

3500 BC Cave-dwelling tribes of *Ciboney* and *Gauanahatabey* inhabit Cuba.

1200 AD *Taíno* arrive in Cuba.

1492 Columbus lands on the north-eastern coast.

1496 Columbus returns on second voyage and explores southern coast.

1508 Sebastián de Ocampo circumnavigates the colony. The Spanish realise Cuba is an island.

1512 Diego de Velázquez founds Baracoa.

1512-15 Six garrison towns are established: Santiago de Cuba, Bayamo, Puerto Príncipe (Camagüey), Sancti Spíritus, Trinidad and Batabanó.

1517-19 Spanish expeditions leave Cuba to search for gold in Mexico.

1519 Garrison port of San Cristóbal de la Habana moved to present site of Havana.

1523 Santiago de Cuba is proclaimed capital of the colony.

1524 First large slave shipment arrives.

1538 Pirate raids devastate Havana, slaves rise up and sack the city.

1542 Spanish crown abolishes slavery of Indians.

1548 Cultivation of sugarcane begins. Spaniards import more Negro slaves.

1550 Indian serfdom outlawed by Spanish crown.

1558 Havana becomes the colony's capital.

1717 Tobacco growers begin armed insurrection against Spanish trade monopoly.

1741 English occupy Guantánamo for five months.

1762 English occupy Havana and make it a free port.

1763 English return Havana to the Spanish in exchange for Florida.

1770 English import more than 10,000 slaves to work on plantations.

1783 Spanish import 100,000 African slaves.

1790-2 Haitian slave revolt makes Cuba the centre of Caribbean sugar production.

1821-5 500,000 slaves imported to Cuba.

1844 *La Escalera Rebellion* - a period of barbaric Spanish repression.

1845 Slavery is abolished internationally, but not in Cuba.

History (Continued)

1853-73 130,000 Chinese arrive as indentured labourers.

1848 US Government offers Spain $100 million for Cuba. The offer is rejected.

1879-80 General Calixto García leads independence uprising known as the Small War.

1886 Cuba is the last island in the Caribbean to accept the abolition of slavery.

1895-98 Second War of Independence, organised by José Martí and led by Antonio Maceo and Máximo Gómez.

1898 USA declares war on Spain when USS *Maine* is sunk in Havana Harbour. Spanish colonial forces withdraw from Cuba.

1898-1901 US military government runs Cuba.

1901 Constitution drawn up. Platt Amendment gives the USA the right to intervene in Cuba's domestic affairs. US investment increases rapidly.

1902 Cuba achieves semblance of independence. Republic of Cuba proclaimed. Tomás Estrada Palma becomes President. US forces leave Cuba.

1903 USA negotiates naval bases at Bahía Honda and Guantánamo Bay.

1909 José Miguel Gómez becomes second President.

1913 Mario García Menocal becomes third President.

1920 So-called 'dance of millions' - a period of short-lived prosperity founded on skyrocketing sugar prices.

1921 Alfredo Zayas y Alfonso made President.

1924-5 Gerardo Machado elected President.

1927 Machado extends Presidential terms, dictatorship begins.

1933 General strike. Machado flees.

1934 Batista orchestrates coup d'etat.

1934 Platt Amendment revoked. USA takes 99-year lease on Guantánamo Bay.

1934-40 Batista rules through puppet presidents.

1940 New constitution ratified. Batista elected President.

1944 Batista defeated in elections by *Auténticos*.

1952 Batista seizes power. Corruption and repression reach new heights.

1953 Castro leads failed attack on the Moncada barracks.

1955 Castro exiled to Mexico.

1956 Castro and Ché Guevara land in Cuba with over 80 men aboard the yacht *Granma*.

History (Continued)

1959 Batista regime crumbles and he flees to the Dominican Republic. Castro made Prime Minister. Constitution suspended.

1960 US businesses in Cuba nationalised. Exodus of Cuban bourgeoisie to Miami.

1961 US-trained Cuban exiles stage abortive invasion at the Bay of Pigs. USA severs diplomatic relations and imposes trade embargo. Castro states Cuba's Revolution is socialist.

1962 Soviets install nuclear missiles in Cuba. US President John F Kennedy instigates naval blockade. USSR agrees to withdraw missiles.

1963 Cuba expelled from Organisation of American States at US bidding.

1965 Cuba Communist Party (PCC) formed. Ché Guevara resigns from the government.

1967 Ché Guevara shot and killed in Bolivia.

1968 Final wave of nationalisation eradicates private enterprise.

1971 Cuban poet Heberto Padilla arrested for 'cultural crimes against the Revolution.

1975 First Cuban troops deployed in Angola to help Marxist government.

1980 125,000 Cubans leave for USA in Mariel boatlift.

1985 Official inauguration of anti-Castro Radio Martí.

1989 Cuba withdraws from Angola. Collapse of the USSR.

1990 Angolan war hero General Arnaldo Ochoa is executed by Cuban authorities.

1991 Soviet troops withdraw from Cuba.

1992 The Cuban Democracy Act extends trade embargo to US subsidiaries.

1993 Castros daughter and granddaughter flee Cuba for the USA.

1994 UN calls for US trade embargo to be lifted. Anti-Castro demonstrations in Havana. USA overturns practice of granting asylum to Cuban refugees.

1995 Castro travels to the USA where he addresses the UN General Assembly. The Pope calls for an end to the embargo. Cuban Foreign Minister Robert Robaina visits Australia in an attempt to cement closer economic ties between the two countries. Castro visits China and Vietnam.

subsisting primarily from shellfish, wild fruits and iguanas. They had only the most rudimentary tools and no domestic utensils. In fact, the *Guanahabateys* were so elusive that the Spanish believed they had tails.

By the end of the 15th century, the *Ciboney* were confined to the south coast, and the *Guanahatabey* to pockets on the north coast. Both tribes had been ousted from other parts of the island by the neolithic *Tainos*, a more advanced Arawak tribe who migrated to the Caribbean from the area between the Amazon and Orinoco basins in northern South America. The *Taíno* constituted around 80% of the population of Cuba at this time. They arrived from what is now the Dominican Republic in the 12th century. A second wave arrived in the 15th century, only a few generations before the Spanish.

The sedentary *Tainos* were a peaceful, friendly people with a well-developed social and cultural life. They held festivals to worship their ancestors, feasted, danced, sang, played ball games on rectangular quads, smoked tobacco, got drunk on fermented cassava, and slept in hammocks - no wonder Columbus was initially so taken with them.

Spanish Conquest

Columbus arrived at Cayo Bariay on Cuba's north-eastern coast on 27 October 1492, labouring under the misapprehension that he had found a western route to Asia. He was impressed by Cuba, recording in his log that he 'had never seen such a beautiful place', and promptly sent men ashore with letters mistakenly addressed to the Japanese emperor.

The *Tainos* welcomed the Spaniards, feasting them with cassava bread, introducing them to tobacco and syphilis, and enriching the Spanish language with words such as barbecue, cigar and hàmmock. But this did little to offset the disappointment Columbus felt when the gold, spices and fabled riches of the East Indies were not to be found.

Columbus spent five weeks exploring the northern coast of Cuba and returned on a second voyage in 1496 to sail the length of the southern coast. To his dying day, he believed that Cuba was attached to the Asian mainland - a gaff so risible now that it detracts from his 'discovery' of a continent ripe for European exploitation.

In 1508, two years after Columbus' death, Sabastian de Ocampo circumnavigated Cuba, and in 1511 the eldest son of Columbus contracted Diego de Velázquez to conquer the island for Spain. Velázquez sailed from neighbouring Hispaniola with 300 men and took just a year to secure the island and quell Indian resistance.

In 1512, gold was found in central Cuba and Spaniards arrived in droves from Hispaniola. The indefatigable Velázquez subsequently founded garrison towns in Baracoa, Santiago de Cuba, Bayamo, Puerto

Príncipe (Camagüey), Sancti Spíritus, Trinidad and Batabanó, but by 1519 the gold deposits were exhausted. When Hernando Cortés sailed from Cuba to conquer Mexico, the Spanish switched their attention to the mainland, leaving Cuba trampled, degraded and depopulated.

The Downfall of the Indians

There were between 50,000 and 100,000 Indians in Cuba when the Spanish arrived, but it took only two generations to destroy their cultures. Spanish brutality was amply recorded by the tracts of the Dominican priest Bartolemé de las Casas, who warned the colonists that they would burn in hell for their sins against the Indians. But the Spanish did not purposely commit genocide; they were keen to have the Indians work for them.

The Spanish, quite obviously, had not come

Hatuey and the Indian Resistance

The legend of Hatuey still exerts a strong influence in Cuba, partly to heroize the Indian resistance and the conquest of the Spaniards, and partly because it's the name of a popular Cuban beer. Hatuey was an Arawak chief who fled to Cuba from Spanish-occupied Hispaniola. Fully aware of the implications of the conquistadors' arrival in Cuba, he besieged Velázquez's expeditionary troops at Baracoa for two months, using guerilla tactics to attack the better armed but phlegmatic force.

When Hatuey was finally captured, Velázquez ordered that he be burnt at the stake. According to legend, he was offered the chance to die by the sword if he converted to Christianity, but responded with the dignified riposte: 'If torture and murder are the wishes of your God, I cannot be part of that religion and I cannot see myself enjoying heaven with such men who obey the cruel wishes of such a God. Are there any Spaniards in Paradise? In which case I have no wish to be seen there myself'.

to the Caribbean to exert themselves. Castilian imperialism was based on military heroism and honour, not manual labour. To develop the new colonies, settlers were assigned Indian serfs in a system known as *encomienda* - a form of slavery in everything but name. In essence, the Indians were forced to work for nothing in return for being civilised by their masters and introduced to the word of the Lord.

However, the Indians were not physically strong and not used to hard labour. When they were taken from their villages to the gold

Hernan Cortés

Hernan Cortés was the epitome of the ruthless, swashbuckling, amorous conquistador, and his exploits have become the stuff of legend.

Renowned for conquering Mexico and overthrowing the mighty Aztec empire, Cortés' meteoric rise to power began in Cuba when he joined Vel- ásquez's expeditionary force. For his part in the successful campaign, Cortés was made clerk to the treasurer, and then elected major of the then capital of Cuba, Santiago de Cuba. After two ill-fated Spanish attempts to establish a presence on the American mainland, Velásquez appointed Cortés to lead a third expedition to Mexico. The speed with which he raised 11 ships and 600 followers roused so much jealousy that his appointment was rescinded, but Cortés hurriedly put to sea before he could be replaced. He arrived off the Yucatan coast in 1519 and burned all his ships to ensure his mutinous troops were committed to conquest. His military victories on the mainland gave him power over an enormous territory, and drained Cuba of settlers. Ultimately, it was the riches the conquistadors found on the mainland that ensured Cuba's future as a staging post for goods shipped back to Spain.

mines in central Cuba, they were overworked and dispossessed of seafood (the Indians' main source of protein). Their lack of resistance to European diseases decimated their ranks. Some tribes died fighting the Spaniards, while others were unconvinced of the benefits of hard work and Christianity and committed mass suicide.

The Catholic Church and the Spanish crown philosophically opposed enslavement: the former championed the rights of the Indians, the latter attempted to regulate the encomienda system. Although Indian serfdom was abolished by the Spanish crown in 1542, the high-minded legislation was compromised by local interests in Cuba and little changed.

Some historians claim the Indians were extinguished by 1570, but this appears unlikely. Spanish-Indian relationships were widespread and the *mestizo* offspring were classified as 'white' in later Spanish censuses. Recent historians have suggested that the pure Indian population still constituted 10% of Cuba's population as late as the mid-17th century, and has gradually been absorbed. This would account for the large number of Indian words which infiltrated the Cuban Spanish language.

Piracy

When the Spanish found the gold and silver they dreamt of in Mexico and South America, Cuba became a staging post for goods being shipped back to Spain. Havana's strategic importance grew when Spain's European rivals began attacking Spanish ships and ports in the Caribbean. For the next 150 years, England, France and Holland considered freelance and government-sanctioned piracy a legitimate and effective way to share in Spain's New World trade.

The Isla de la Juventud (Island of Youth) and the north coast of Holguín Province became favoured haunts of buccaneers. This was the fabled lawless era of Blackbeard, Calico Jack, Anne Bonney and Henry Morgan - pirates who plied the Spanish Main attacking flotillas, picking off stray vessels, and plundering ports. In response to the attacks, the Spanish ships sailed in armed convoys, meeting in Havana once a year before setting sail for Seville. Havana thrived by resupplying ships and entertaining crews who waited months for convoys to gather.

The Spanish belatedly fortified their Caribbean ports after the French Corsair, Jacques de Sores, captured Havana in 1555 and burnt the nascent settlement to the ground. Havana's El Castillo de la Real Fuerza was completed in 1577 and repelled English sea-dog Francis Drake in 1588. Havana and Santiago de Cuba got more forts over the next 20 years but the rest of Cuba was neglected, and pirate raids on coastal towns did nothing to encourage development.

The Spanish Monopoly

Spain maintained an economic stranglehold on Cuba for the next two centuries, through the regulations of the Casa de Contratación. The Casa, established in 1502, registered, licensed and effectively monopolised trade and immigration to the New World. It collected taxes on imports and exports, ruled on commercial matters in the colonies and made nonsensical decrees such as that requiring all goods from the New World to be channelled through the mediocre port of Seville. Its attempts to manage trade slowed the growth of Cuba, stifled the export of tobacco and sugarcane, led to widespread smuggling, and legitimised the plundering of the Indies by jealous and excluded European powers.

In the 18th century, Cuba was buffeted by the side effects of wars between the European superpowers.

When the Spanish commissioned privateers to attack British ships smuggling slaves to Cuba, it sparked the so-called War of Jenkins' Ear. The British seized Guantánamo Bay in 1741 and made unsuccessful attacks on Santiago de Cuba and Havana. They were more successful during the Seven Years War, when a colossal fleet sailed to Havana in 1762, stormed the fort, and occupied the city for a year. Although the primary aim was to use Havana as a bargaining chip in peace talks, the British lifted all trading restrictions and irrevocably altered the course of Cuban history.

Havana experienced a fiftyfold increase in trade. Some 700 merchant ships descended on the city in a single year, compared to a maximum of 15 each year for the previous decade. The potential of free trade with the American colonies to the north was engraved on the Cuban consciousness. The British exchanged Havana for Florida in 1763, but the insularity of Spanish rule had been broken. The impetus for this evolution was sugar and slaves.

Sugar and Slaves

Sugar had been grown in Cuba for over 200 years but compared to the French and British sugar islands in the Caribbean, its production was paltry, technologically backward and lacking cheap labour. The Spanish had no direct access to the African slave markets, and contracts to supply slaves to Cuba had been strictly controlled by the Spanish crown. Slaves made up less than half of Cuba's 70,000 strong population in 1762, whereas they outnumbered settlers by five or 10 to one on British and French Caribbean islands.

The British imported more slaves during their year in Havana than had been imported in the past decade. The sugar industry took off during the American War of Independence when Spain encouraged Cuba to trade with Britain's rebel colony, and Cuba became the USA's main sugar supplier after 1783. Spain facilitated growth by relinquishing its monopoly on the supply of slaves. The 1790 slave revolt in Hispaniola led to an influx of experienced plantation owners, giving Cuba the three prerequisites for its sugar boom - markets, labour and technological know-how.

Slave traders invested in Cuba's burgeoning sugar industry, cementing the symbiotic relationship between slavery and sugar. Sugar prices rose dramatically at the end of the 18th century, leading to the construction of 200 mills in Havana over the next two decades. There was no shortage of labour, despite Spain's agreement in 1817 to abolish the slave trade by 1820. More than 100,000 slaves were imported to Cuba between 1816 and 1820, and the weakened Spanish crown was in no position to enforce abolition. Instead, it relaxed trade restrictions and opened Cuba to ships of all nationalities, setting the stage for the momentous surge in the Cuban economy.

Opposite
Calle Obispo
Havana

Cuba's wealth for the rest of the 19th century was dependent on sugar and slavery. The sugar boom between 1821 and 1865 saw 500,000 African slaves brought to the island. The harsh slave regime, by then illegal, survived because of the enormous wealth it generated and because of the bribes paid to Cuba's captain-generals not to enforce anti-slavery legislation.

By 1849, Cuba had become the largest sugar producer in the world, supplying over a fifth of the world's sugar. For the planters in Havana, this was a period of opulence and extravagance. Apocryphal stories abound of gin and eau de cologne on tap in the bathrooms of Havana's palaces, while open sewers ran in the street outside. But in the midst of this excess was the gnawing reality that the sugar boom had come late to Cuba, and the slavery on which it depended was an outdated institution withering in the face of international humanitarianism.

Stirrings of Autonomy

In the mid-19th century, Cuba's planters and merchants conspired to prolong slavery - the basis of their wealth. There was constant fear of a slave uprising like that in Haiti, especially since blacks outnumbered whites for the first time in the island's colonial history. The planters were also anxious that Spain might be persuaded to enforce anti-slavery legislation and require Cuba to free the 500,000 slaves imported since the banning of the slave trade in 1820. Flirtatious moves were made to the USA to sound out its feelings on annexation, which the planters considered the safest way to preserve the status quo. The alternative was a bloody push for independence, which would disrupt the Cuban economy and might provoke Spain to emancipate the slaves in defence of its colony.

Annexation was not a fanciful dream. The USA had been Cuba's largest trading partner for 20 years, dominating 80% of the island's trade. It had recently won California and New Mexico, and bought Louisiana and Florida. There were plenty of unfulfilled US expansionists who considered Cuba as rightfully belonging to the Union. The USA made three attempts to buy the island in the middle of the century, backed up by veiled threats that invasion was imminent. The offers (between $100 and $130 million) were considered but rejected.

Slavery was clearly not going to last in Cuba, so Spanish peasants, indentured Canary Islanders and Chinese were imported as alternative sources of labour. Many of the richest planters in the west of Cuba began to seek reforms, and pushed for political representation to ensure that compensation would be forthcoming if emancipation was declared.

The reform movement stagnated and the political initiative passed

Opposite
Booksellers in
Old Havana.

The Body Count

Like most other military adventures in Cuba, the greatest cause of death in the Second War of Independence was disease, especially in the concent- ration camps. Three hundred thousand Cubans lost their lives in the three-year conflict - over 15% of the population. The Spaniards lost 53,000 men to disease and a little under 10,000 in battle. The US lost only 650 in battle but almost ten times that number to disease. For a while it looked as if the US incursion would fail because of the large number of troops succumbing to yellow fever and malaria. During the peace treaty negotiations, the high death rate among US personnel in Cuba made it uncertain whether the new superpower would be able to maintain its hold on the island.

to the less wealthy landowners in the east, who were still unmechanised and lacked the benefits of the railway. The eastern planters were heavily reliant on slave labour, and the price of slaves had risen so dramatically since the slave trade ended in 1865 that they could no longer afford to buy them. Unable to afford new slaves or to mechanise their mills, they were in danger of becoming obsolete. The Havana planters had too much to lose to lead a revolt, but this was not the case in the east.

The Ten Years War

The uprising took place in Bayamo in October 1868, led by the landowner Carlos Manuel de Céspedes, who freed his 30 slaves and commanded an army of 147 men into action. Within a month, the rebel army had swollen to some 12,000 men, many of them free blacks attracted by Céspedes's act of emancipation. The army captured Bayamo and Holguín, and new revolts broke out in Puerto Príncipe. By the end of the year, Céspedes found himself in control of a rebel republic.

Although the uprising has been painted as a pro-independence, abolitionist revolt, it hedged its bets on the slavery issue and its primary initiative on Cuba's constitutional future was to once more court annexation by the USA. In many respects, the war turned into a fight between Cuban-born creoles and Spanish-born peninsulares: the former pro-independence, the latter loyal to the Spanish crown. The conflict between the two groups had simmered for two hundred years, fuelled by creoles' resentment at exclusion from high office and Spain's unwieldy control of Cuba's trade. The fortunes made by the peninsulares during the sugar boom had only intensified the antipathy.

The Spanish had only 7000 troops on the island at the time of the uprising, but were swiftly reinforced by *peninsulares*, civilians who formed semi-vigilante groups called Volunteers. The Volunteers organised an army of 33,000 men and together with 40,000 Spanish troops had contained the rebels by 1869.

Céspedes and his commanders, the *mulatto* Antonio Maceo and the Dominican Máximo Gómez controlled the east, but the west remained in Spanish hands and continued to harvest record sugar crops. The rebels used classic guerilla tactics, roaming the countryside in small bands, avoiding the better armed Spanish military and attacking mills and sabotaging infrastructure. The Spanish responded by declaring martial law, rounding up the inhabitants of several large cities into concentration camps, and giving the Volunteers a free hand in committing atrocities whenever the urge took them.

The rebels looked to US support and the *peninsulares* to strong Spanish commitment, but neither was forthcoming. The island slid into a state of anarchy as the rebels changed their tactics and announced their intention to burn the sugar estates in the west. The Spanish responded by digging a fortified ditch across the entire island, sealing off the rebel stronghold of Oriente Province.

Tactical disagreement among the rebels led to Céspedes being replaced, but in 1875, Gómez got his way, crossed the fortified ditch into central Cuba and burned 83 plantations around Sancti Spíritus. When Gómez was repelled, rebel morale and financial support began to decline, and many rebel leaders deserted or surrendered. An armistice was signed in February 1878, but Maceo refused to accept its terms and sailed into exile. The war was estimated to have cost a quarter of a billion US dollars, and to have claimed over 200,000 Spanish and 50,000 Cuban lives.

Between the Wars

Although Cuba's sugar industry escaped the war unscathed, it suffered a series of shocks in the peace that followed. Sugar prices plummeted, German sugar beet ate into Cuba's European markets, and a dearth of capital, since the high-rolling days of the slave trade were over, left plantation owners up to their eyeballs in debt. A central system developed which saw those with access to capital build large, technologically advanced mills supported by private railroads. The mills bought cane from the surrounding planters, who simply became primary producers in an increasingly mechanised and sophisticated process.

The decline of Cuba's oligarchic class and the need for new capital left a vacuum filled by US money and influence. Not only did US companies purchase Cuban sugar estates, but the Cuban sugar industry became almost totally reliant on US sugar imports.

Meanwhile, slavery came to a subdued end in 1880, without compensation to slaveholders. A decree gave slave owners the right to keep slaves for the next eight years under a system of apprenticeship, but most relinquished the right, correctly believing that contract labour was cheaper. By 1886, 90% of slaves had been freed and the apprenticeship system was abolished two years early.

During the 1890s, the most progressive political force in Cuba was the Autonomist party, a middle class movement which sought self-rule for Cuba within the Spanish empire. When political reforms failed to materialise and *peninsulares* retained the top jobs, the onus shifted to the revolutionary pro-independence lobby, most of whom were in exile in the USA.

The Fight for Independence

The most prominent pro-independence activist was the remarkable poet, journalist and philosopher José Martí. In 1892, he founded the Cuban Revolutionary Party, which was dedicated to establishing a politically and economically independent republic through revolution. Aware that Spain was a declining power in the region, Martí warned against encroaching US imperialism in Latin America, and tried to unite the splintered Cuban nationalist groups by transcending issues of race, class and gender. He organised support among Cuban exiles in New York and tobacco workers in Florida, founded a pro-independence newspaper, organised revolutionary training camps in Florida, and collected 10% of Cuban exiles' salaries to finance the cause. To achieve his goal, Martí recruited Antonio Maceo and Máximo Gómez, the military leaders of the Ten Years War, and fomented local uprisings in Cuba.

Martí, Maceo and Gómez sailed to Cuba in April 1895. The island was ripe for rebellion. High taxes and tariffs, and a decline in sugar prices had caused economic hardship. Although US capital was modernising the sugar industry, profits were no longer staying in Cuba. Tension between the *creoles* and *peninsulares* was high, and there was widespread corruption among *peninsulares* officials. The war began with a series of popular uprisings. Martí attempted to create a civilian rebel government but was killed in one of the first skirmishes, leaving the military leaders in control of the campaign.

The rebels fought a guerilla war, operating in small bands, living off the land and avoiding engagement with Spanish forces. Rebel numbers were not large, wavering between 8000 and 25,000 over the three years of the war, but they were supported by virtually the entire rural population and received money, supplies and arms from exiles in the USA. Armed with little more than machetes, they burnt their way across the country, torching both Cuban and US-owned plantations and mills. It was assumed that Spain would not fight hard to hold onto an economically ruined Cuba.

The Spanish captain-general, Valeriano Weyler, declared martial law, hounded rebels with military patrols, re-fortified cross-country ditches used in the Ten Years War and rounded up over 300,000 peasants into concentration camps. After three years of gruelling fighting, the Spanish began to regain military control. The rebels were ragged and dispirited by the death of several leaders, including Maceo, and had failed to achieve US recognition of their rights as belligerents. The Spanish government had captured the political initiative by declaring autonomy and establishing a government of reformers and autonomists in Havana.

The wild card in the conflict was the continuous spectre of possible US involvement. The US government was eventually hounded into the war by expansionist interests and the hysteria whipped up by the gutter press. Public sentiment was personified in the bellicose figure of the then American Under-Secretary of the Navy, Theodore Roosevelt, who was keen to prove himself in action, test his new navy and forge the US national character in the heat of combat. Cuba looked like a likely cause and Spain a willing victim.

To prevent the USA entering the conflict, Spain assented to every US demand - including granting universal suffrage in Cuba - but it was not enough. The USA made a last-ditch attempt to purchase the island and then took up the burden of their manifest destiny.

The USS *Maine* was sent to Cuba, ostensibly to protect US interests, and when it was blown up in Havana Harbour with the loss of 255 American lives, war was almost certain. The Americans blamed the Spanish; the Spanish hinted that the Americans had destroyed the ship as a pretext for invasion. After an inconclusive inquiry, the USA declared war on Spain in April 1898.

The 'Spanish-American War' (referred to by Cubans as the 'Cuban-Spanish-American War') was short, one-sided and farcical, but it signalled the rise of the USA as a new global power. The entire Spanish Pacific fleet was destroyed off the Philippines in under an hour without a single US casualty. The Atlantic fleet was blockaded in Santiago Harbour by the much superior US navy, while US troops landed 25km east at Daquirí. Cuban rebels helped secure the terrain around Santiago de Cuba. When the US cavalry and infantry stormed San Juan Hill on the outskirts of Santiago de Cuba, the myth of Roosevelt (now deputy commander of a cavalry regiment) and his Rough Riders was cemented forever in the US imagination. In truth, 700 deflated Spaniards held up 6000 US troops and inflicted such heavy losses on them that 10% of the US invasion force was dead or wounded in a matter of hours.

When the Spanish fleet was decimated trying to ram its way out of Santiago Harbour, the Spanish surrendered and the American flag was raised over Cuba. Rebel forces were excluded from the city for fear of reprisals and took no part in the peace treaty negotiations held later in Paris. It would not be the last time US actions aroused resentment among Cuban nationalists.

Spain granted independence to Cuba. Over the next three years, Cuba was ruled by a US military government which disarmed the rebels, initiated elections, and supervised the writing of a constitution. Before full independence was granted, the US congress passed the Platt Amendment, giving the USA ownership of the Isle of Pines (renamed Isla de la Juventud after the Revolution), the right to

José Martí

José Martí was an acclaimed poet, playwright, journalist, philosopher, orator, political activist and, finally, a revolutionary martyr. He orchestrated Cuba's second war of independence and was the main theoretician of Cuban revolutionary thought.

Martí was born into a poor Havana family in 1853. He edited a pro-independence school paper and was sentenced to six years hard labour - he was only 16 - for criticising a schoolmate for attending a pro-Spanish rally. He spent six months breaking rocks in a quarry, before being transferred to the Isla de la Juventud and deported. He spent the next two decades in exile in Spain, Mexico, Guatemala and the USA, writing plays, poems and newspaper articles championing the cause of Cuban independence.

In 1892, Martí founded the Cuban Revolutionary Party, which was dedicated to establishing an independent republic through revolution. He subsequently raised money for an invasion among Cuban exiles in New York and tobacco workers in Florida. He landed on the south coast of Oriente Province in 1895 and after five weeks of inconclusive engagements was killed while riding his horse into a skirmish in Dos Rios. Martí was 42 years old.

Martí is today probably the most honoured man in Cuba. Every town has a street, monument or building named after him. Havana's airport is called the José Martí International Airport. Martí's birthday, January 28, is a Cuban public holiday. The USA has also gotten into the act, and called its propaganda radio station which is broadcast into Cuba, Radio Martí.

establish naval bases in Cuba, and the right to intervene in Cuba's domestic affairs if it considered such a move prudent. José Martí had been right all along.

The Stillborn Republic

After four centuries of Spanish colonialism, Cuba proved to be infertile ground for enlightened concepts such as democracy and republicanism. For the next 50 years, Cuba's governments were characterised by graft, corruption and electoral fraud.

Economically, Cuba became a client state of the USA, whose investment in Cuba topped US$1.5 billion in 1925, and the island was totally reliant on US sugar imports to sustain its domestic economy. The fragility of this single market monoculture became apparent as the world price of sugar and the level of US tariffs caused repeated booms and busts. Cuba was politically bound to the USA by the Platt Amendment, which was invoked to support US military incursions in 1906, 1912 and 1917-21.

A series of corrupt and uninspiring presidents came and went. Many Cubans despaired of achieving progress through the republic or under the yoke of US economic imperialism. The emergence of the authoritarian General Machado y Morales in 1924 - who, in the process, turned Cuba into a one-party sate, quashing the nascent labour movement - marked a new low in Cuban politics, but the USA was loath to intervene again in Cuban affairs.

The worldwide depression in the 1930s bankrupted Cuba and led to widespread civil unrest. Machado's stranglehold on political debate led to student activism and the emergence of shadowy terrorist organisations. Cuba became awash in violence as terrorist cells and Machado's henchmen slaughtered each other, pushing the republic into anarchy. The USA finally used its political clout to persuade Machado to stand down. During the general strike of August 1933, Machado saw reason and fled to the Bahamas under a hail of gunfire, beginning the tradition of hurried exits by Cuban presidents who had outstayed their welcome.

Machado's departure did nothing to quell the violence, which spiralled out of control. Into the power vacuum stepped Fulgencio Batista, a 32-year-old army sergeant, who managed temporarily to align the army and the radical students - the two most potent forces in Cuban politics. Batista solidified his control of the army and proved himself ruthless and powerful enough to regain a semblance of order. Relieved that anarchy had been suppressed, the USA did not protest Batista's coup. Although it refused to recognise the first of Batista's puppet presidents, it rewarded Batista by annulling the Platt Amendment and reducing tariffs that were hurting Cuba's sugar

Dope Inc

Charles 'Lucky' Luciano was the brains behind the Mafia becoming the most powerful and feared criminal syndicate in the USA. He also ensured Cuba became one of the world's most important transit points for heroin after WW II.

Quick to seize any opportunity, Luciano made the decision to take the Mafia into the profitable - and still nascent - heroin trade after Prohibition came to an end in 1933. He entrusted Meyer Lansky, a prominent Jewish criminal, to oversee the Mafia's financial empire, and organise distribution. It proved a remarkably good choice: Lansky's knowledge and clout in the Caribbean and especially his ties with the Florida-based hoodlum Santo Trafficante Jr, meant heroin could pass, relatively unchecked, through Cuba or Florida on its way to the USA.

Luciano travelled to Cuba in 1947 - Havana's role in the international drug trade was complete. By the early 1950s, Luciano's mobsters were flying in, clinking cocktails and bragging about how 'safe' Havana had become. They did have a point: most of the hotels and casinos were controlled by the Mafia; the government looked skyward to business which brought badly needed capital; and Santo Trafficante Jr, a close friend of the dictator Batista, controlled much of the booming tourist industry.

However, the Revolution in 1959 meant any further operations were stalled. Castro nationalised foreign-owned businesses, forcing the Mafia to abandon their lucrative casino operations. Although heroin continued to be bought into Miami, another narcotics transfer point had opened up that was taking attention away from Cuba: the Golden Triangle in South-East Asia.

In the mid-1980s, Castro became increasingly linked to the fugitive drug financier Robert Vesco, who settled in Havana in 1982. According to the *New York Times* in 1984, Vesco was spending $50,000 per day in Havana, providing Cuba with a valuable source of foreign exchange. (A man of legendary largesse, he once gave his bodyguards Rolexes so they wouldnt be late for work.) But in June 1995, Vesco was taken into custody after his relationship with the government 'turned difficult'.

Interestingly, he is among 91 fugitives living in Cuba that the US has tried unsuccessfully to extradite in recent years.

exports.

Support for Batista's progressive policies was so widespread in Cuba by 1940 that he held free elections and won resoundingly. He oversaw the ratification of a popular liberal constitution and continued to rule throughout the boom years of World War II. Things were looking so rosy by 1944 that he was tempted to repeat his flirtation with democracy. This time, to his surprise, he was defeated, but stepped down graciously. Two more presidents came and went, fleecing the nation of staggering amounts of money during the sugar booms.

The disenchanted Cuban electorate was poised to elect the progressive Orthodox party in the 1952 election when Batista seized power a second time. The returning Batista was almost unrecognisable from the people's champion a decade earlier. He aligned himself with mercantile rather than proletariat interests, and began to rule without regard for democratic or judicial niceties. Batista siphoned $300 million into overseas accounts over the next six years from racketeering, bribery and abuse of the lottery. His police force quashed opposition with a disregard for the law that institutionalised gangsterism. Abuse of the electoral system, widespread torture and assassination, and US willingness to support his regime kept him in power until 1958, when the tired, mistreated and disillusioned populace looked to Castro's revolutionaries for release from the tyranny.

The Emergence of Fidel Castro

During the 1950s, a number of radical movements had sought to supplant Batista. Foremost among them was an organisation led by a mercurial lawyer and admirer of José Martí named Fidel Castro. On 26 July 1953, the 26-year-old Castro and a group of some 150 men (including his brother Raúl) stormed the Moncada barracks in Santiago de Cuba. But the assault was spectacularly unsuccessful: most of the attackers, including the Castro brothers, were mowed down or imprisoned by Batista's forces.

The brouhaha surrounding the attack attracted immediate media attention, and much emphasis was placed on the harsh treatment meted out to the prisoners. Fortuitously for Castro, the coverage helped push his nascent organisation to national prominence and it was soon seen as a legitimate political threat.

At his subsequent trial, Castro denounced corruption, arguing that his actions were fuelled by nationalism, social justice and the need for Cuba to return to democratic government. His famous speech, concluding with the line *'La historia me absolverá!'* ('History will absolve me!'), was hardly revolutionary - though it did contain radical demands - but its appeal and piquancy struck a sympathetic chord with many Cubans.

Castro was imprisoned on the Isle of Pines (now the Isla de la Juventud) then pardoned by Batista in 1955. He travelled to Mexico where he established the 26th of July Movement (the name is derived from the date of the Moncada barracks assault). Soon after, he was joined by a young firebrand called Ernesto 'Ché' Guevara. Born in Rosario, Argentina, in 1926, Ché trained as a doctor before undertaking a tour through the poorer regions of Latin America. The pairing proved opportune; they quickly hatched a plot to return to Cuba and topple the Batista dictatorship.

Revolutionary Cuba

After military training and raising funds for goods and equipment, Castro and over 80 men sailed from Mexico on the yacht *Granma* (apparently a misspelling of Grandma) for the shores of Cuba. They landed on 2 December 1956 at a swamp on the south-west coast of Oriente Province, close to the Sierra Maestra mountains. Much like the Moncada insurrection, the attack proved a shambolic and costly affair: lead astray by hostile peasants, set upon by inclement weather and ambushed by Batista's soldiers, most of the bedraggled rebels were either caught or forced to flee. Some, including the Castro brothers, took refuge in the Sierra Maestra where, over time, they regrouped, winning converts among the dirt-poor locals as well as forcing victories against the government troops.

But it was slow going. By 1958, neither the guerillas in the Sierra Maestra nor the

> ## Where There's Smoke There's Fire
>
> During the 19th and early 20th centuries, rollers at the cigar factories would often be entertained by men reading aloud books and magazines. These 'readers', as they were called, were also entrusted with educating the tobacco workers. Through their judicious selection of material, the readers were instrumental in pushing many workers into supporting the independence movement - even playing a small role in Castro's rise to power in the late 1950s.

vigorous (if divided) urban arm of the organisation - made up of workers, students and conservative Catholic officials - had made much headway against Batista. However, a series of articles published in the USA by *New York Times* journalist Herbert Mathews - likening Castro to a freedom fighter pitted against a venal dictatorship - engendered enormous benefits to the rebel movement. The US decision in 1958 to suspend arms sales to Cuba was also telling. At home, Batista's popularity plunged as he laboured to convince Cubans that his government was a creditable alternative to the one championed by Castro.

Batista realised his government was doomed unless he could rout the guerillas once and for all. On 24 May 1958, Batista mounted an all-out offensive against Castro's guerillas. However, his forces were badly undone: scuppered morale created paralysis within the ranks and this, coupled with all-too-frequent insurrections, lead to the army's eventual defeat.

On 1 January 1959, Batista conceded defeat and fled Cuba for the Dominican Republic. His departure was immediately followed by the arrival of Ché Guevara and the Fidelistas, who marched into Havana to a heroes' welcome. The victorious Castro entered the city a week later.

The Revolution's Aftermath

Joyous celebrations and Castro's realisation that changes - socially, politically and ideologically - were needed to retain public support, marked the period immediately after Batista's flight. With alacrity and energy, the revolutionary government proposed a series of sweeping reforms: reducing rents, improving social services, nationalising large holdings of land, regulating foreign interests, increasing wages and salaries, and increasing industrialisation.

At the same time, opposition to the regime - most notably from the Catholic Church, former comrades, anti-communists and pro-democracy figures - was being increasingly stifled. The press was censored, the electoral process was phased out and many Cubans, primarily drawn from the middle classes and soured by the government's new directions, left the island for the USA.

Further hopes for a democratic transformation began to fade as Castro moved increasingly towards an alliance with the USSR.

US-Cuban Relations during the 1960s

Relations between the two countries became parlous in the early 1960s when Cuba began to commandeer US-owned interests such as oil refineries and sugar plantations, and nationalise that country's mining, financial and hotel operations. The situation was further exacerbated by US suspicions of Castro, especially after democratic elections had been cancelled, communist activity had increased, and the summary executions of a number of Batista's supporters became public.

In 1960, under the nose of an apoplectic USA, Soviet Foreign Minister Anastas Mikoyan arrived in Havana; a deal was quickly

The Role of Women in Cuba

Cuba up until the 20th century was a male-dominated society with women playing decidedly subordinate roles. But their status was considerably enhanced by the Revolution's zeal for greater social and sexual equality.

On 23 August 1960, the female network which had contributed so diligently to the rebel effort - often in the frontline, women organised medical supplies, administered treatment to the wounded, and taught schools while the guerillas were esconced in the Sierra Maestra mountains - was officially founded as the Federation of Cuban Women (FMC). It has since become the most important and influential national group advancing the status of women. Membership still remains coveted (nearly 80% of Cuban women belong), conferring merit to those who join.

Women have understandably taken hold of their opportunities, leading the push for literacy and achieving sporting, cultural and military success (Cuban women fought in Angola from 1975 to 1988). They are also well represented in professional fields, although few hold government positions in the PCC. Child-care facilities are freely available throughout the country and there is legislation in place that requires men to share equally in domestic chores and child-rearing if a wife is working for the benefit of the state.

struck between the two countries which granted Cuba a credit of $100 million to purchase much-needed technology. Soon after, trade agreements were also clinched with Poland and China.

The Bay of Pigs

The USA, under President Eisenhower, broke off all diplomatic ties with Cuba in January 1961. Determined to quell any 'unfriendly' regimes near its borders, the USA had allowed - with the co-operation of the Central Intelligence Agency (CIA) - the covert training and equipping of Cuban exiles in Guatemala the year before, in preparation for an overthrow of Castro. (A number of other ludicrous attempts had been made to eliminate him, including a plan to blow him up with a booby-trapped cigar.) But its execution was a fiasco. Castro and his troops were already aware of the invasion, while strong anti-Castro sentiment inside Cuba - heavily banked on by the CIA - proved a furphy.

The invasion force of almost 1300 men landed at the Bay of Pigs on 15 April 1961. President John F Kennedy, reluctant to expose his hand in the cauldron of Cold War animosity, failed to sanction US air cover from ships stationed off the Bay of Pigs. Denied aerial support, the invading brigade was easy pickings for the Cuban troops (led by Castro's brother Raúl), and mopped up within three days. The captured exiles were later exchanged for food, medicine and heavy machinery.

Crushing the invasion amounted to a significant victory for Castro, which only strengthened his control. Furthermore, it helped push Castro, who had announced that he was a Marxist-Leninist, well and truly into the Soviet corner.

The Cuban Missile Crisis

In October 1962, US reconnaissance planes confirmed the presence of nuclear missiles on Cuba. Their discovery sparked another major confrontation with the USA. The Soviet premier Nikita Kruschev had assumed that the USA would tolerate the deployment of medium and intermediate-range ballistic missiles on the island - an incredible oversight when you consider Cuba is only 145 km from the US mainland. (Kruschev had given their installation the green light after assurances to Castro that he would defend Cuba with Soviet weaponry.) President Kennedy reacted by placing a naval 'quarantine' on Cuba, and demanded that the missiles be immediately withdrawn.

After six days of coronary-inducing brinkmanship when war seemed certain, Kruschev backed down. He informed Kennedy that no further sites would be built and that any missiles remaining in Cuba would be dismantled and shipped back to the USSR. The USA in return agreed not to attempt any further invasions of Cuba. Infuriated by the Soviet backdown, Castro - courting conflagration - vowed to shoot down prying US planes but, muzzled by the Soviets, was powerless to act.

The crisis marked the end of a splenetic period in US-Soviet relations; it also increased the friction between Cuba and the USA.

Prioritisation and Consolidation

Among the priorities of the government in the early 1960s was the cementing of its power and the addressing of Cuba's long-standing sugar-dependent economy. Both could be achieved, the government argued, by agricultural diversification and a re-emphasis on industrial programs. By doing so foreign revenue would significantly increase, internal demand would be met and a range of heavy industry could be introduced. Ché Guevara, who was appointed head of the National

The New Man

'We will make the man of the 21st century: we ourselves'.
Ché Guevara

On the urgings of Ché Guevara, Cuba's leaders began to embrace the view that their version of socialism could only succeed if a new society and a 'new socialist man' were created - the antipode of the *homo economicus* of capitalism.

Commitment to the new social reforms was paramount. Unwillingness to conform to this model and its prototypes - Castro, Guevara and the guerillas of the 1956 campaign - often meant ostracism, mob harassment and sometimes imprisonment.

Bank and the Ministry of Industries, set about implementing a Four Year Plan (the tenet of which was the overhauling of the economy by Soviet-inspired central planning). Cuban workers were now exhorted to achieve production targets for purely selfless reasons - and not for material or individual benefit.

Unfortunately, the push towards manufacturing proved problematic as it impinged on the export agriculture that had previously buoyed economic growth. In addition, the US embargo with Cuba had severely curtailed the flow of technical and financial supplies needed to kickstart the governments industrial programs. Cuba was therefore forced to turn to the USSR for assistance. Industrialisation was also hampered by the Cuban leaderships feckless grasp of administrative and production planning, which affected economic performance and stunted its overall development.

Chaos was the unplanned result. The successful redistribution of income which occurred in the early years of the Revolution meant items that had previously been available only to the rich were suddenly in general demand. The system simply couldn't cope; in 1962, rationing was introduced, prompting queues (*la cola*) in towns and cities throughout the country. Soon, even basic goods became scarce. By 1963, Cuba's Soviet-block benefactors had had enough, and demanded an immediate return to that mainstay of the economy - sugar. Reluctantly, the Cuban government agreed.

Castro subsequently declared that 10 million tons of sugar - almost three million tons more than the next largest haul - would be harvested by 1970, and that millions of Cubans would be mobilised to achieve this goal. Anything less would be deemed a failure.

In 1965, the Cuba Communist Party (PCC) was unveiled. Castro appointed himself first secretary of the PCC, as well as the prime minister and chief of the armed forces. Daily political life intensified as individual goals were relegated to the greater good of the state.

The response of the people during this time was mixed. Some chose to leave the country (which stripped Cuba of vital skills and expertise when it was most needed) while the majority, despite their privations, continued to support the government. Since the Revolution, the quality of life had vastly improved: food and housing was widely available, and there was universal access to social services. Education became a major priority, and literacy rates rose to 95%. Racial cleavages were also redressed and the status of women enhanced. For many, these were new and challenging times: exciting, intoxicating, full of future promise.

In 1970, Castro was forced to

The Death of Ché Guevara

Ché Guevara left Cuba in 1965. His aim: to fan the flames of revolution in other countries. He journeyed to help rebels in the Congo, then went to Bolivia, which had been embroiled in radicalism since the 1950s.

In 1967, when the USA was involved in the Vietnam War, he blazingly declared his hopes of 'creating a second or third Vietnam' and to transform the 'Andes into another Sierra Maestra'. His outbursts put a price on his head; shortly after, he was captured and executed by US-trained Bolivian Rangers.

admit defeat - only eight and a half million tons of sugar had been reaped. Although a record yield, the 10 million benchmark had not been achieved. To make matters worse, tobacco production was also down. For Castro and the Revolution, the resulting shortfall was a difficult pill to swallow. Not only had it damaged the government's credibility, it had also highlighted Cuba's inability to achieve economic sovereignty.

Survival at a Cost

Cuba turned increasingly to the USSR for financial aid and assistance. In return, the Soviets attempted to revamp the island's economy. They proved moderately successful: productivity slowly rose and by the early 1970s, small businesses were again allowed to operate. Exports also increased and the tourist sector was greatly expanded.

Furthermore, the trade embargo imposed by the USA was relaxed in the mid-1970s, which led many to believe that the mutual hostilities between the two countries had been put aside. Unfortunately, rapprochement between Cuba and the USA was abruptly dashed once Cuban troops were sent to support the Marxist-backed government in Angola. As a result, US President Gerald Ford vowed to further tighten economic restrictions.

Disenchantment with Castro's government, both nationally and overseas, also became evident during the 1970s and 1980s. In 1971, the noted poet and academic, Heberto Padilla, was arrested for committing 'cultural' crimes against the Revolution and was forced to confess his transgressions in public. Howls of outrage greeted the incident and many writers, including Jean-Paul Sartre, Mario Vargas Llosa and Octavio Paz - who had previously embraced the objectives of Castro and the Revolution - sprung to Padilla's defence. Castro, however, was unmoved. In a speech soon after Padilla's arrest, he made his position abundantly clear: those who weren't for the Revolution were against it.

By 1980, the political situation within Cuba had grown worse. In that year, 11,000 people sought political asylum in the Peruvian embassy in Havana. Castro responded by opening the port of Mariel allowing those who wished to leave the island the chance to sail by small craft to the USA. Almost 125,000 *marielitos* (Mariel refugees) set out.

Compounding Cuba's problems was once again its worsening economic performance, especially during the latter half of the 1980s. Even though the USA never managed to impose its unilateral blockade on other countries, there was still only a small trade with non-COMECON nations such as Spain, Mexico and Argentina for basic items and US-manufactured goods.

Facing an Uncertain Future

With the collapse of communism and the breakup of the USSR in 1989, Cuba has stagnated. Oil supplies have been lost, trade has dwindled, and the country's domestic economy has been crippled. Agricultural machinery has been replaced by oxen (Cuba is presently in the fourth year of the largest conversion of any nation in history from conventional modern agriculture to large scale organic farming); food and medicinal supplies have become increasingly scarce; and bicycles have replaced vehicles as the main form of transportation. Without economic assistance (the USSR used to subsidise Cuba to the tune of $500,000 an hour), the government has been unable to meet the standards of living achieved a generation ago.

Ailing national confidence in Castro has also become apparent since

1989. To the disgust of many Cubans, General Arnaldo Ochoa, a decorated veteran of the Angolan campaign, was executed in 1990 for his alleged involvement in diamond and drug running. On 21 December 1993, Castro's daughter, a vocal critic of the government, fled to the USA. She was followed ten days later by Castro's granddaughter. And on 5 August 1994, thousands of people converged in Havana shouting '*Abajo Fidel*' ('Down with Fidel') on what became the first anti-Castro rally since he came to power.

But mindful of his deleterious position, Castro has reluctantly agreed to reform. In order to help the island emerge from its slump, he has sought investment from overseas (even for sugar, once the symbol of Cuban nationalism); passed laws which allow foreigners to own 100% of their enterprises (instead of a 50% partnership with the state); encouraged private employment and small businesses; opened a number of 'dollar stores' where only US dollars hold sway; and encouraged the growth in tourism (currently a windfall). Other cure-alls designed to stimulate the economy, as well as reduce Cuba's level of debt to Western nations, include cuts in the bureaucracy, the introduction of income tax, a convertible currency, and the slashing of state subsidies on many goods and services. Possibly the most far-reaching change has been the establishment of open markets, in which small-scale producers can sell agricultural and industrial goods.

Fingers crossed that free-market reforms and foreign investment can help maintain his grip on power and 'save cradle-to-grave Cuban socialism', Castro has courted, among others, fashion designers Luciano Benetton and Pierre Cardin - who has established a factory and retail outlet on the island - French auto giant Peugeot, Mercedes Benz, and Australia's Western Mining Corporation, who have entered into a US$500 million joint venture with Cuba.

Already more than 30 Spanish firms have begun operations in Cuba and recently a Mexican telecommunications company brought a 49% share in the Cuban state telephone company. Even the USA has agreed with Cuba on reciprocal media rights in their respective countries. And late in 1994, 69 US companies held talks with Cuban officials with a view to begin trade and investment 'whenever it becomes possible'.

And yet, the lifting of the embargo by the USA seems as far away as it has been since its inception in 1961. The Clinton administration has pooh-poohed suggestions that the embargo should be lifted; rather it defends its position that changing US policy when Castro's government is bowed and almost broken is naive. (The Cuban Democracy Act of 1992, popularly known as the 'Toricelli Act' after its sponsor, congressman Robert Toricelli, effectively extends the embargo to US subsidiaries.) In addition, the role played by the powerful Cuban-American lobby led by Jorge Mas Canosa - courted by both Republicans and Democrats alike - has been extremely influential in shaping Clinton's resistance to scrapping the freeze.

The US government also overturned the practice, begun in 1966, of welcoming almost any Cuban who could manage to get to its shores; instead, refugees were taken to its naval base at Guantánamo Bay. Aimed at countering the increasing numbers of *balseros* escaping from Cuba to the USA, the legislation had little impact: on one day in 1994, more than 3000 *balseros*, some in bathtubs, were scooped up and rescued - the largest airlift in a single day since the Mariel exodus of 1980.

It was only when a deal between the two countries was struck that some semblance of normalcy returned: the USA promised to accept an annual quota of at least 20,000 immigrants so long as Cuba stopped illegal ones setting to sea.

Early in 1995, members of the US Congress pushed to further tighten the economic embargo against Cuba. The Republican Senator Jesse Helms introduced legislation that sought to strengthen broadcasts of the anti-Castro TV *Martí* to Cuba, and prevent anyone from entering the USA that had, in any way, profited from the confiscation of US property in Cuba by Castro's government. He was quoted as saying at the time that 'whether Mr Castro leaves Cuba in a vertical position or horizontal position does not matter. But he must, he will, leave Cuba'. Contrasting all this was the formal recognition of Vietnam - subject to a similar debilitating embargo - by the USA a few months later.

In hindsight, perhaps too much emphasis has been placed on Castro and the Revolution. If current shortages are overcome, the promise of higher living standards are fulfilled and the USA considers denting key parts of the embargo such as trade with and travel to a once US-dominated market, then the Cassandras of the regime will be silenced; on the other hand, if economic relief is not achieved, the socialist state built by Castro and the Revolution may no longer be sustainable.

For this country and its ageing leader, the greatest challenge is still to be faced.

Geography

Cuba lies at the entrance of the Gulf of Mexico, only 145 km from the US mainland. It is the largest island in the Antilles Archipelago, with a total land area of 110,860 sq km (slightly smaller than the US state of Pennsylvania). The island's overall length from east to west is approximately 1200 km long while its average width is just under 100 km.

Cuba has a variegated topography that includes rugged mountains, rolling hills, lush valleys, vast plains, bays, beaches, swamps and rivers. Covering 25% of the island from east to west are three distinct mountainous regions: the Oriental (which has the 1972-metre Pico Turquino, Cuba's highest peak); Central; and Occidental ranges. Tropical lowlands and basin areas occupy the remaining 75% of land supporting rice, fruit, sugar and coffee plantations, and livestock. Cuba's largest river is the Río Cauto, which stretches 261 km across the eastern part of the island.

Climate

Cuba's climate, moderated by trade winds, is subtropical with over 330 days of sunshine per year. Temperatures are generally pleasant, rising to 34 °C in summer and dropping to 21 °C in winter. The warmest months are July and August (average temperature is 30 °C) while the coldest month is January (average temperature is 25 °C). The best time to visit Cuba is during the dry season from November to April.

For swimmers and water-sports enthusiasts, the average annual coastal water temperature is a soup-like 26 °C.

Humidity, with an annual average of 75%, tends to make things sticky in Cuba. The hot, wet season is from May to October, with rainfall heaviest in the mountains which receive up to 2500 mm a year. The driest months are February and March. Havana's average annual rainfall is 1224 mm.

Flora and Fauna

Cuba's national flora is the ubiquitous royal palm. The country is also home to over 8000 plant species including the prehistoric *parma corcho* (cork palm), *mariposo* (butterfly jasmine) and beautifully coloured orchids.

The national bird is the *tocororo*, which has distinctive red, white and blue plumage - the colours of the Cuban flag. Cuba's other bird species include bee hummingbirds (the smallest bird in the world), nightingales, woodpeckers, owls and flamingoes.

The island possesses a wide variety of animal life with deer, wild boar, alligators, iguanas, pygmy boa constrictors, and the *almiqué*, a tiny mammal with a large proboscis, making up just some of the species. There is also a profusion of marine fauna found in Cuba's waters including crocodiles, manatees, beaked fish, lobster and shrimp while a great variety of coral (especially black coral) hug the island's edges.

Government

Cuba is a socialist state and governed by the PCC. The highest authority is the National Assembly; from its ranks the Council of State is appointed, the chairman of which is Chief of State and Head of Government. This has been, since February 1959, Fidel Castro (first as prime minister then as president). His brother Raúl ranks immediately below.

Local government is divided into municipal and provincial administrative divisions, based on a council system, with the municipalities being subordinate to the 14 provinces - Pinar del Río, La Habana, Ciudad de la Habana, Matanzas, Cienfuegoes, Villa Clara,

Voices of Dissent

It is almost impossible to give precise estimates of the number of political prisoners (called *plantados*) held by the Cuban government. In the main, this is due to the severe restrictions on human rights monitoring within the country, and because of lack of official information. However, it could be argued that during times of national crises such as the Bay of Pigs invasion in 1961, imprisonment was more widespread than it is today. Castro stated in 1965 that the government held 20,000 political prisoners but some sources in the early 1970s pushed that figure towards 200,000 - making Cuba a veritable Latin American Gulag.

By the mid 1970s, the number had dropped considerably with around five thousand prisoners held in Cuban gaols. Castro later expressed a willingness to release more which was vindicated in a report by the Inter-American Commission on Human Rights (IACHR) that estimated only 1000 political prisoners remained in Cuba. However, as noted by the commission, those still incarcerated were subject to intimidation, mistreatment and were consistently denied adequate medical treatment. Prisoners who expressed their opposition to the regime and regarded rehabilitation as anathema to their beliefs were particularly singled out for harsh treatment.

In the 1990s, many more political prisoners have been released with most making their way to the USA. Cuba insists that there are now no prisoners of conscience but some, such as Amnesty International, refute this, believing as many as 500 remain behind bars.

Sancti Spíritus, Ciego de Avila, Camagüey, Las Tunas, Holguín, Granma, Santiago de Cuba, Guantánamo - and the special municipality of Isla de la Juventud.

Population and People

Population

Cuba's population totals 11 million with almost 70% living in the country's cities. The city of Havana has the largest population with 2,200,000, followed by Santiago de Cuba with 1,100,000.

People

Over 50% of the Cuban population is mulatto, 37% European, 11% Black and 1% Chinese and Asian.

Arts and Culture

Music and Dance

The popularity and influence of Cuban music has been profound this century. Its reach has extended to the infiltration of 'mambo', 'rumba' and 'cha-cha-cha' into the popular lexicon to the salsa boom which swept the world in the 1970s, and which shows no sign of letting up in the 1990s.

Cuban music is characterised by decorous vocalisation, melodic harmonies, and the use of stringed instruments. The introduction of African slaves to the island meant that drums, an exceptionally fluid song form and a vocal style where participants call and respond, were also added to the mix.

Internationally renowned musicians include Celia Cruz (now in exile), Israel 'Cachao' Lopez (long billed as the inventor of mambo), jazz/Latin fusionists Irakeré, 14-member dance band Los Van Van and the son band Sierra Maestra.

Rumba

The rumba is thought to have originated in Matanzas Province in the early 1900s. In style it is imitative of ballroom dancing, and involves a series of dances where the male partner salaciously thrusts his pelvis in the direction of the female. The songs, featuring lots of percussion, are usually performed by a soloist with the accompaniment of a small chorus.

Contradanza

The *contradanza* is modelled on dances that were popular in the rural areas of France, and most likely arrived in Cuba with the large Haitian immigration in the period 1914-18.

Salsa

A type of Latin American big-band dance music popular in Cuba, *salsa* has been a worldwide sensation (especially the USA) for over two decades. Actors Andy Garcia, Robert Duvall, Sharon Stone, Sandra Bullock and Marlon Brando are fans, while Albita Rodriguez (a former nightclub singer from Cuba) is slated to be the next crossover star in the USA.

Son

A blend of African and Latin American influences, *son* is thought to have originated in Cuba's eastern provinces. The style, renowned for its often stirring vocalisation and hypnotic chorus, is one of the most resilient and popular forms of music in the country.

Cha-cha-cha

Enrique Jorrín, a violinist born in the city of Pinar del Río, was the founder of the cha-cha-cha. A Latin American twist on the ballroom dance, the style incorporates breezy vocals and an unorthodox instrumental arrangement. The Historical Museum in Pinar del Rí features a display on the life and work of Jorrín.

Abakúa

Abakú was introduced to Cuba during the slave trade, having originated from the Negebe people of West Africa. Rhythms, often played on a lead drum held under the arm, are repetitive, and according to one practitioner, 'mind bending'.

Mambo

Part jazz, part music of the big band era, *mambo* uses lots of brass instruments, and is distinctive for its tight arrangements and African influences.

Bolero and Filin

Both styles are a syncretism of classical Spanish and Italian operas, lachrymatic ballads and gentle solos. They're understandably popular with older Cubans, but sneered at by the younger generation.

'Nueva' Trova

This musical form, inspired by The Beatles, Bob Dylan, Joan Baez, Pete Seeger and the clarion calls of the Revolution, rose to national prominence in the early to mid-1970s. The beat is laidback and folksy; the lyrics a blend of the poetic and the earnest. The *Case de la Trova*, in Santiago de Cuba, is the country's foremost venue for this style.

Discography of Cuban Music

Cuban sounds worth investigating include:

Los Munequitos de Mantanzas	The Rumba Originals
Beny Moré	El Bárbaro Del Ritmo
Celina Gonzales	Fiesta Guajira
Orquesta Ritmo Oriental	La Ritmo Oriental te Estâ Llamando
Los Van Van	Songo
Orquesta Revé	La Explosión Del Momento
Sylvio Rodríguez	Cuban Classics
Carlos Puebla	Traigo de Cuba un Cantar
Joseíto Fernández	Homenaje Póstumo
Sierra Maestra	Grandes Exitos
Irakeré	Irakeré En Vivo
Various	Latin Roots
Various	Viva! El Rito
Various	Sabroso - Havana Hits
Various	A Carnival of Cuban Music

Film

There are plenty of Hollywood movies about Cuba, although you could be forgiven for thinking that the country ceased to exist after New Year's Eve 1958. Included among them are enough films covering the collapse of the Batista regime for a whole iconography of the Cuban Revolution to have developed. They invariably include Batista's New Year's Eve farewell speech, a snapshot of Fidelista guerrilla activity and the gleeful smashing of parking meters by a jubilant Havana population.

A better representation of Cuban life is found in the films of the director Tomás Gutiérrez Alea (*Death of a Bureaucrat*, 1966, *Memories of Underdevelopment*, 1968, and more recently *Strawberry and Chocolate*, 1993). Other popular Cuban films include *Lucia*, which examines the changing roles of women from colonial times to the present, and the cartoon feature *Vampires in Havana*.   Unfortunately, despite support from the government, the national film industry has crept along with lemur-like pace as the economic crises has made film stock extremely scarce. New movies are, therefore, few and far between.

Filmography of Cuba

Cuban Rebel Girls (Barry Mahon, 1959)
This dreadful movie about a gaggle of beautiful girls fighting for the Revolution is a must for all Cuban cineastes. Not only is it Errol Flynn's final movie, it was also filmed in 1959 in Cuba with the assistance of Castro's army. A stupendous PR disaster.

Our Man in Havana (Carol Reed, 1960)
Likeable but confused adaptation of Graham Greene's oddly prescient novel about a Havana vacuum cleaner salesman recruited as a spy. Makes good use of the intrigue, mistrust and suspicion prevalent in pre-revolutionary Havana. Alec Guiness bumbles his way through the plot in familiar Ealing comedy mode. Noel Coward plays a commendable supporting role.

Death of a Bureaucrat (Tomás Gutiérrez Alea, 1966)
One of the best comedies ever made and a good tribute to the director's raft of cinematic heroes - Charlie Chaplin, Laurel and Hardy, et al. The film also has a mean edge, and cruelly sends up the Dudley Do-Rights that barnacle every revolution, especially the one at home.

Godfather II (Francis Ford Coppola, 1974)
A section of this elegiac family history covers the Mafia's move offshore into Havana's gambling and hotel interests in the 1950s. Beautifully shot in washed-out colours, the film is especially memorable for the Havana rooftop scene where the Meyer Lansky character slices and shares a birthday cake decorated with a map of Cuba. This is a good portrait of anything-goes 1950s Havana, showing the Batista government working hand-in-hand with organised crime. The Cuban sequences were shot in the Dominican Republic.

Cuba (Richard Lester, 1979)
A portrait of the Revolution seen through the eyes of a British mercenary hired to co-ordinate Batista's counter-insurgency strategy. The film provides a lacerating picture of Havana's decadent upper class and the corruption-riddled Batista regime, but ultimately degenerates into a sub-James Bond action farce, replete with *Fidelastas*. Have they ever been cornier?

Scarface (Brian de Palma, 1983)

In-your-face, malevolent portrait of an unpleasant Cuban Mariel emigré who makes it to the top of the Miami crime world only to be brought down by his Latin machismo, nihilism and incredibly bad taste in couture. Includes documentary footage of the Mariel boatlift, scenes in a Miami refugee holding camp, and a comic appraisal of the Cuban *paisan* (countryman) coming to terms with US social mores.

Havana (Sydney Pollack, 1990)

A $50 million flop (it returned only $5 million) of Casablanca transposed to 1958 Cuba, with Robert Redford playing the apolitical American who finally gets down off the fence because his love interest is involved in the revolutionary struggle. The film successfully highlights the climate of fear during Batista's second reign, with the secret police working overtime harassing dissidents. There's a couple of eyebrow-raisers though - Batista is depicted as blond (he was black) and a nincompoop (he had written three books). Its satisfying nonetheless, with plenty of bodies being dropped out of moving cars to enliven proceedings.

Mambo Kings (Arne Glimcher, 1992)

Hollywood bio-pic formula movie about two oleaginous Cuban mambo musicians trying to crack the big time in 1950s New York. The film is saved only by the fantastic soundtrack, suave costumes and Celia Cruz, the Queen of Salsa in Havana in the 1940s. Based on the Pulitzer Prize winning Oscar Hijuelos novel *Mambo Kings Play Songs of Love*.

A Few Good Men (Rob Reiner, 1992)

A tight, military courtroom drama which reveals the siege mentality of US personnel in Cuba and the Cold War-warrior mindset favoured by those who believe such outposts are the frontiers of Western civilisation. Let down only by the fact that the characters played by Tom Cruise and Demi Moore are held up as exemplars of truth, justice and US liberalism.

Strawberry and Chocolate (Tomás Gutiérrez Alea, 1993)

Engaging film of social manners that gently manoeuvres through a range of contentious issues: gay politics, Cuban notions of tolerance, revolutionary ideals. There's some great scenes of Havana (especially Vedado, the Malecón, and the Coppelia ice-cream parlour) plus plenty of throwbacks to 1970s fashion. A big favourite at international film festivals when first released.

Recommended Reading

Politics
Face to Face with Fidel Castro: A Conversation with Tomás Borge (Ocean Press, 1993) by Fidel Castro.
Eyeball to Eyeball: The Inside Story of the Cuban Missile Crisis (Random House, 1991) by Dino Brugioni.
Deadly Secrets: The CIA-Mafia War Against Castro and the Assassination of JFK (Thunder Mouth, 1992) by Warren Hinckle.
Family Portrait with Fidel (Random House, 1984) by Carlos Franqui.
Castro's Cuba, Cuba's Fidel (Westview Press, 1990) by Lee Lockwood.

History
The United States and Cuba: Business and Diplomacy, 1917-1960 (College and University Press, 1960) by Robert F Smith.
Cuba or the Pursuit of Freedom (Eyre & Spottiswoode, 1971) by Hugh Thomas.
Cuba - A Short History (Cambridge University Press, 1993) by Leslie Bethell.
Reminiscences of the Cuban Revolutionary War (Penguin Books, 1969) by Ché Guevara.
Guevara (Fontana, 1970) by Andrew Sinclair.
Revolution in Cuba (Scribners, 1965) by Herbert Mathews.
Cuba: Between Reform and Revolution (Oxford University Press, 1988) by Louis A Pérez Jr.
Cuba 1933: Prologue to Revolution (Cornell University Press, 1970) by Luis A Aguilar.

General
Three Trapped Tigers (Harper & Row, 1971), *Infantes Inferno* (Faber & Faber, 1979) and *Mea Cuba* (Faber & Faber, 1994) by Guillermo Cabrera Infante.
Our Man in Havana (Heinemann, 1958) by Graham Greene.
The Old Man and the Sea (Scribners, 1952), *To Have and Have Not* (Macmillan, 1962) and *Islands in the Stream* (Scribners, 1970) by Ernest Hemingway.
Old Havana, Cuba (Tauris Parke Books, 1990) edited by Nicolas Sapieha.
Roll Over Ché Guevara: Travels of a Radical Reporter (Verso, 1994) by Marc Cooper.
The Emergence of the Latin American Novel (Cambridge University Press, 1977) by Gordon Brotherston.
Falling Off the Map (Knopf, 1993) and *Cuba and the Night* (Knopf, 1995) by Pico Iyer.
AfroCuba: An Anthology of Cuban Writing on Race, Politics and Culture

(Ocean Press, 1993) edited by Pedro Pérez Sarduy and Jean Stubbs.
Cuba, Que Bola! (Clique Publishing, 1995) by Tania Jovanovic.
Cuba in Focus: A Guide to the People, Politics and Culture (Latin American Bureau, 1995) by Emily Hatchwell and Simon Calder.

Language

Spanish is Cuba's official language though English and a smattering of French and German are spoken at hotels and tourist areas.

Useful Words and Phrases

hello	hola
yes	sí
no	no
Good morning	Buenos días
Good afternoon	Buenas tardes
Good evening	Buenas noches
What's up?	Que hola?
goodbye	adiós
thank you	gracias
please	por favor
My name is...	Mi nombre es.../Me llamo...
How do you do?	Cómo está usted?
I don't understand	No entiendo
Do you speak English?	Habla usted inglés?
I don't speak Spanish	No hablo español
Help!	Socorro!
How much is...?	Cuánto cuesta...?
Its very cheap	Está muy barato
Its too expensive	Está demasiado caro
Last person in the queue?	Ultimo?
(you ask this when waiting for a bus)	
I don't want anything	No quiero nada
I'm not rich	No soy rico
soap	jabón
credit card	tarjeta de crédito
I was cut off	Me cortaron la linea
the cigar box isn't any good	los tabacos no son buenos

Directions

Where is...?	Dónde está...?
room	cuarto
money exchange	casa de cambio
airport	aeropuerto

bus station	terminal de omnibus
train station	estación de ferrocarriles
ferry terminal	embarcadero
ticket office	taquilla
post office	correo
hospital	hospital
petrol station	gasolinera
How far?	A qué distancia
I'm lost	Estoy perdido/a

Days of the Week

Sunday	domingo
Monday	lunes
Tuesday	martes
Wednesday	miércoles
Thursday	jueves
Friday	viernes
Saturday	sábado

Time

What time is it?	Qúe hora es
morning	mañana
yesterday	ayer
today	hoy
tomorrow	mañana
week	semana
month	mes

Numbers

one	uno/una
two	dos
three	tres
four	cuatro
five	cinco
six	seis
seven	siete
eight	ocho
nine	nueve
ten	diez
twenty	veinte
fifty	cincuenta
one hundred	cién
one thousand	quinientos/as
one million	millón

Food

rice	arroz
bread	pan
toast	tostada
vegetables	vegetales
salad	enselada
sandwich	bocadito
ice cream	helado
eggs	huevos
omelette	tortilla
cheese	queso
pork	cerolo
rabbit	conejo
lamb	corolero
hamburger	hamburguesa
ham	jamón
lobster	langosta
prawn	langostino
goose	oca
turkey	pavo
fish	pescado
chicken	pollo
veal	ternera
fruit	frutas
guava	guayaba
orange	naranja
pineapple	piña
bananas	plátanos
grapefruit	toronja

Learning Spanish

If you wish to improve your Spanish, the University of Havana, Calle San Lazaro y L, Vedado, ph 78 3285, runs an intensive language, cultural and historical course over three weeks at the beginning of the year. Accommodation is provided at the Colina Hotel nearby. The Universidad de Oriente also runs similar courses in Santiago de Cuba. A comprehensive list of where to study Spanish can be obtained from any Cuban embassy.

Religion

Roman Catholicism has traditionally been the dominant religion and is still the largest denomination with 47%. An estimated 4% of the population are Protestant while almost 2% are Afro-American Spiritist.

There is also a small Jewish population in Havana.

Catholicism

Cuba was comfortably Catholic up until the Revolution. But by the early 1960s, relations between the Catholic Church and the state had deteriorated as the church sought to restrain Castro's *caudillo* (political strongman) temperament. Many clergy members found themselves on his wrong side and were subsequently deported. Castro's desire to secularise religion soon left its mark: church attendances fell; religious holidays were scrapped; Catholic schools were nationalised; and the priesthood waned. Church authorities referred to the period as the 'silencing of God'.

However, in the 1980s, the state began to actively encourage closer ties between itself and the Cuban Catholic Church. Services have since increased, new churches have been built and other Christian denominations are being recognised. In 1991, religious adherents were also permitted to join the PCC.

Speculation mounted in late 1995 that Pope John Paul II intended to visit Cuba, the only Latin American country he has yet to set foot in. This would be an unexpected coup for the Cuban government, and its reward for improving relations with the Holy See (the Archbishop of Havana, Jaime Lucas Ortega y Alamino, is a cardinal).

Santería

A derivative of Catholicism introduced by the Spanish and mixed with the African religions brought to Cuba by black slaves, *Santería* loosely means 'the way of the gods'.

This reconciliation occurred when slaves identified their deities with colour rather than human figures (they would therefore worship the colours in which the saints were clothed). For instance, Our Lady is dressed in white, so in Santería she becomes Obatala; Our Lady of Regla is dressed in blue, thus becoming Yemaya; Our Lady of Charity is dressed in yellow, so is Ochun, etc. Santería festivals are causes for great celebration, with participants dancing, singing, beating sacred *batá* drums, performing rituals and sacrificing the odd animal.

The government has recently promoted the growth of cultural and religious interest in Afro-Cuban practices and it's not uncommon to see PCC members openly wearing Santero devices.

Festivals and Holidays

The irresistible Varadero (January/February), Santiago de Cuba (July) and Havana (July also) carnivals are major drawcards for Cubans and travellers alike. Other festivals include: the sparkling New Latin American Film Festival (Havana, December); the Jazz Festival (Havana, February); the Varadero International Music Festival (Varadero, November); the Ballet Festival (Havana, November); and a slew of smaller celebrations with revellers strutting, skipping and dancing in the streets over the New Year.

Official national holidays include:

Anniversary of the Revolution - January 1
International Labour Day (May Day) - 1 May
Anniversary of the Moncada Barracks Attack - July 26
Anniversary of the beginning of the Wars of Independence -
October 10

Entry Regulations

A valid passport and a Cuban visa (or Tourist Card, which is available from travel agencies, tour operators or the Cuban Consulate) are necessary for most foreigners entering the country. Both are valid for stays of up to one month; passports are not stamped but tourist cards are. Extensions of a month can be obtained from the larger hotels or travel agencies (this process is relatively straightforward). Travellers arriving in Cuba as transfer or transit passengers are allowed to remain in the country for up to 72 hours without a visa or tourist card.

It's advised that you keep excellent care of your tourist card. (I was detained, then admonished by airport authorities as I was about to leave Cuba. The reason? My card had worn at the edges.)

The USA prohibits its citizens from travelling to Cuba unless they're journalists, academics, clergy members or diplomats. However, this has recently been tightened and now all US citizens must have a licence. Specific licences on a case-by-case basis for humanitarian travel (eg cases of extreme hardship relating to close relatives) are also considered. US citizens should contact the Cuban Interests Section, 2630-2639 16th Street NW, Washington DC 20009, ph (202) 797 8518 for more information.

Customs

Officially, travellers to Cuba are allowed to bring two bottles of alcohol, one carton of cigarettes per adult plus cosmetics and medicine. However, these limits are rarely adhered to. A prescription should also be carried if you are travelling with medication. Illegal drugs are prohibited in Cuba as are animal foodstuffs, plants, seeds, vegetable produce, weapons, munitions, poisons, films, written documents or material that could 'undermine the political, social and economic situation of the country'.

Exit Regulations

International departure tax is $12.

Embassies

Foreign embassies in Havana include:
Argentina, Calle 36 No 511 e/ 5ta y 7ma, Miramar, ph 33 2573.
Australia, No representation. Refer to Australian Embassy in Mexico City. Ruben Dario 55, Esquina Campos Eliseos, Col Polanco 11580, Mexico, D.F. ph 525 531 51225
Austria, Calle 4 No 101, Miramar, ph 33 2825.
Belgium, 5ta Ave No 7408, Miramar, ph 33 2410.
Brazil, Calle 16 No 503, Miramar, ph 33 2139.
Canada, Calle 30 No 518, Miramar, ph 33 2516.
France, Calle 14 No 312 e/ 3ra y 5ta Ave Playa, Miramar, ph 33 2132.
Germany, Calle 28 No 313 e/ 3ra y 5ta, Miramar, ph 33 2539.
Italy, Calle Paseo No 606 e/ 25 y 27, Vedado, ph 33 3334.
Japan, Calle N No 62, Vedado, ph 33 3454.
Mexico, Calle 12 No 518 e/ 5ta y 7ma, Miramar, ph 33 2142.
Netherlands, Calle 8 No 307, Miramar, ph 33 2511.
Spain, Calle Carcel No 51, Old Havana, ph 33 8025.
Switzerland, 5ta Ave No 2005 e/ 20 y 22, Miramar, ph 33 2611.
UK, Calle 34 No 708, Miramar, ph 33 1771.
USA, c/o US Interests Section, Calzada e/ L y M, Vedado, ph 33 3551.

Money

The peso is the Cuban unit of currency and is divided into 100 centavos. One, two, five, 10, 20 and 40 centavo coins are in circulation. Paper money comes in one, three, five, 10, 20 and 50 peso denominations. Since the Cuban government legalised the use of US dollars in 1993, you will need pesos only for bus fares, local cigarettes, and some foods, such as fruit sold on sidewalks and snacks on train journeys. (When I first tried to pay for a coffee with pesos, the woman behind the counter looked at me as if I was a sex offender.)

At the time of writing, $1 was the equivalent of 30 pesos on the black market.

You might also come across *certificadós de divisa* ('B certificates'). These are the equivalent of US currency and issued in paper money of one, five and 10 dollars and one, five, 10, 25 and 50 cents. Make sure you spend the certificates in Cuba or convert them back into dollars when you depart - the currency is worthless outside the country.

Travellers' cheques (Thomas Cook, Visa etc) are readily cashed at tourist areas and banks, and credit cards including VISA, Diners Club, Eurocard, Access and MasterCard are accepted. Credit cards can also be used to obtain US dollars (advances) from a bank office in the Habana Libre Hotel in Havana. But you can't use any credit card or travellers cheques issued in the USA or by a US bank (that means no American Express).

All prices quoted in this book are in US dollars unless stated otherwise.

Business Hours

Business hours are usually Monday to Friday 8.30am-12.30pm and 1.30-5.30pm. Markets are open 9am-7pm and small shops 8am-1pm, 3-7pm. However, some places, such as museums, can be incredibly capricious, opening and closing as if on a whim (planning a visit in the afternoon, except on Monday when most museums are closed, is probably your best option).

Communications

The ritzier tourist hotels have postal and international telephone services, plus fax and telex machines (sorry, no e-mail). They can also offer IDD (International Direct Dialling). If you want to make an international call outside Havana, think again - Cuba has among the world's least developed telephone systems.

Postcard prices are $0.80 to Europe, Asia, North America and Australasia, and $0.50 to South America. The postal service, both national and international, is practically moribund - you'll likely be home before your correspondence.

An international call is $6 per minute; collect calls are not permitted.

National newspapers in Cuba include *Juventud Rebelde* and *Trabajadores*, published weekly, and the PCC periodical *Granma* (now drastically reduced due to shortages of paper and ink), which is published every day except Sunday. A summary of *Granma* is available every Saturday in English, French, Spanish and German. Cuban magazines include the arty (and very rare) *Bohemia* and the humorous *Palante*. English-language newspapers and magazines such as *Time* and *Newsweek* are few and far between, but they are available from selected hotels (the Habana Libre and the Riviera in Havana) and

Radio

It seems that no one alerted President Reagan and his advisers to the fact that the names chosen for the anti-Castro radio and TV stations that broadcast from the USA to Cuba - Radio Martí and TV Martí - had become synonymous with anti-imperialism. Whether by design or stupidity (I suspect the latter), Radio Martí was officially inaugurated in 1985. It broadcasts news, religious programs and round table discussions in Spanish on everything from human rights to 'album of the week' 24 hours a day (both medium wave and short wave). The name doesn't seem to have vexed the Cubans too much; it is, apparently, the most listened to station in Cuba. TV Martí aired its first broadcast in 1990 and features news, snapshots of life in the USA and major sporting events such as World Series Baseball (in Spanish also). However, massive jamming efforts by the Cuban government makes it difficult to receive the signal in central Havana - or anywhere else for that matter.

In early 1995, Castro moved to restrict unauthorised satellite dishes that were used to receive foreign broadcasts.

stores (see individual chapters for more information).

Two national TV stations, *Cubavision* and *Tele Rebelde,* televise turgid Party propaganda, hideous Brazilian soapies and Hollywood schlockbusters from 6pm to midnight (longer on weekends). The bigger tourist hotels have satellite TV offering CNN, MTV and other English-speaking channels.

Radio stations include radios *Reloj, Progreso* and *Rebelde.* Radio Havana Cuba is the country's only international radio station and broadcasts 24 hours in several languages while Radio *Taíno* broadcasts in Spanish and English throughout Cuba.

Miscellaneous

Electricity
Cuban hotels and tourist offices have two-prong (flat plugs), 110-V outlets and 60 cycles. Blackouts are widespread across the country.

Weights and Measures
Cuba uses the metric system.

Time

The time zone is USA Eastern Standard Time. When it's noon in Havana, it's 4am in Sydney, 11am in Mexico City, 2pm in Buenos Aires, 5pm in London, and 6pm in Madrid and Rome.

Film and Photography

Travellers are allowed to photograph the usual tourist fare such as monuments, buildings, roads, museums, squares, theatres, etc, but are forbidden to film military units or arms, bridges, airports, sea ports, radio stations, and industrial and agricultural plants. It should come as no surprise then that it is also an offence to film from aircraft.

Film is available from major hotels, dollar stores and Photoservice branches throughout Cuba.

Health

Emergency first aid and/or general medical attention is readily available to visitors throughout the country and care is cheap, professional and efficient. Unfortunately, Cuba is presently experiencing shortages and unavailability of some medicines - medical insurance is therefore advised for all visitors. If you intend travelling independently throughout the country, packing a medical kit is also essential.

No vaccinations are necessary although travellers arriving in Cuba from yellow fever zones will have to present a vaccination certificate.

Drinking Water

Filtered water is available from hotels, and bottled water can be bought from hotels, dollar stores and restaurants for around $0.60 for 500ml. Drinking water is also available from dispensers on trains and railway platforms (pack a cup or lidded container for fill-ups).

Health Tourism

With skilled staff and excellent facilities, Cuba has begun to market itself as an ideal health destination. Companies such as Servimed, Calle 18 No 4304 e/ 43 y 47, Havana, ph 22 7023, have health clinics (including accommodation in sometimes stunning surroundings) scattered throughout the country. They treat ailments such as stress, alopecia, melanoma and Parkinson's disease, and they also offer a number of specialised medical courses.

Dangers and Annoyances

Cuba is a remarkably safe destination. While theft (*hurto*) has slowly increased since the recession, it is mostly confined to the filching of cattle, bicycles and car parts (the trade in gas, tyres and windscreens are big business across the island). It pays, however, to take normal precautions with valuables - cameras, handbags etc - left in hotel rooms or when carried around. A common complaint among travellers is that police are often loath to fill out reports for insurance claims relating to theft; be insistent and talk to your travel agent prior to travelling to Cuba.

The reappearance of *jineteras* (prostitutes; the word comes from *jineta* or 'horsewoman') in Havana has become something of a symbol of the Revolution's decline, especially as Castro had sworn to eradicate the profession soon after he came to power. *Jineteras* parade openly on the streets, in restaurants, nightclubs and the lobbies of tourist hotels while *jineteros* (hustlers) pimp, sell drugs and bogus cigars to credulous foreigners, change money or demand soap (strict rationing means Cubans are only allowed one bar of soap each month). Sometimes they're bound to get a fair distance up your nose: 'Hey you! My friend! Change money, buy T-shirt, buy Hatuey beer, you want food, you want taxi, you want a ride on the back of my bike...', on and on it goes.

Work

Volunteer work is available in Cuba. Your own country will have some information. In Australia the Green Team focuses on urban food production. If you're interested and have a background in permaculture and conservation or have plumbing, electrical, carpentry or engineering experience, contact The Green Team, c/- Permaculture Global Assistance Network, The Community House, 6 Derby Street, Kew, Vic 3101, Australia.

What to Bring

Sunglasses, suntan lotion and a brimmed hat are a must but these are readily available in hotel shops or tourist stores. You should also bring besides your personal toiletries, cosmetic supplies, soap, mosquito repellent, the ubiquitous roll of toilet paper, a small medical kit if you intend travelling around the country, a Spanish-English dictionary if you're unfamiliar with the language, beach towels (they are often not supplied by hotels), a small torch in case of power blackouts, and an umbrella, which may prove useful in sudden downpours.

Toothpaste, soap, cosmetics, T-shirts, chewing gum, household medicines and Western music cassettes and magazines, are all appreciated as gifts.

Tipping

Tipping is voluntary but recommended. Usually any tip above 10% of the bill is mouthed with respect and wonder.

Addresses

An Havana address such as Calle 2, No 299 e/ 11 y 13, Vedado means it is numbered 299 and is on the second between 11th and 13th streets. Of course, that doesn't mean you'll immediately find it; in many cases, street signs are non-existent or dwellings/businesses lack any visible number. If you're unsure of a location, ask a passerby for directions.

School Children in Old Havana

TRAVEL INFORMATION

How to get there

By Air

The José Martí International Airport, lying 18km south of Havana, is the main gateway for travellers. Cuba's other international terminals are at Varadero, Cayo Largo, Santiago de Cuba, Camagüey, Cienfuegos, Holguín and Manzanillo.

Cubana, the national carrier, flies to regular destinations in Europe (including Berlin, Brussels, Cologne, Hamburg, London, Madrid, Milan, Moscow and Paris), Canada (Montreal, Toronto and Quebec), the Americas (Buenos Aires, Cancún, Mexico City, Monterrey, Panama City, Río de Janiero, Santiago de Chile, Santo Domingo and Sao Paulo) and the Caribbean (Kingston, Montego Bay).

Aerogaviota, in association with *Cubana*, has passenger and cargo charter flights throughout Cuba as well as the Caribbean and Central America.

Aerocaribbean, a chartered airline, has flights throughout the Caribbean, plus cargo charters to Canada, Mexico, and Central and South America. There are also regular 'charter' flights from Miami but their frequency varies from year to year, depending on political conditions. Unless you're a diplomat, legal immigrant, non-resident Cuban on a 'hardship visit', or a US citizen that has obtained a licence, forget it.

Charter flights are available from Jamaica, Bahamas, Grand Caymans and Holland, plus there is a range of combination flights and package tours from Europe, Australia, Canada and South America (see the following *Tours to Cuba*).

Companies that fly directly to Cuba include:

Aeroflot has flights from Russia (ex Moscow and via Shannon, Eire) to Havana three times a week.

Viasa has flights from England (ex London) to Havana twice a week.

Cubana has flights from England (ex London) once a week.

IW-AOM French Airlines has flights from France (ex Paris) to Havana weekly.

Iberia has flights from Spain (ex Madrid) to Havana daily.

Air Canada has flights from Canada (ex Toronto) to Havana and Varadero weekly.

Canadian Airlines has flights from Canada (ex Toronto) to Varadero weekly.

Cubana has flights from Mexico (ex Mexico City) to Havana twice a week.

Mexicana Airlines has flights from Mexico (ex Mexico City) to Havana five times a week and (ex Cancún) to Havana six times a week.

Copa has flights from Panama (ex Panama City) to Havana five times a week.

Aeroflot has flights from Peru (ex Lima) to Havana twice a week.

Venezolana has flights from Venezuela (ex Caracas) to Havana six times a week.

Caribic Air has flights from Jamaica (ex Montego Bay) to Havana and Varadero weekly.

There are no direct flights to Cuba from Australia or New Zealand; instead visitors have to fly via Los Angeles with stopovers in Mexico or Canada. From Australia, the most convenient route is to fly Melbourne/Sydney to Los Angeles, and from there connect to Mexico City. Another popular route was to fly to Buenos Aires and then on to Havana; unfortunately this is no more as *Aerolineas Argentinas* has stopped its Argentina to Cuba service.

Companies that fly to Los Angeles, Mexico and Canada include:

Qantas has flights from Australia (ex Melbourne and Sydney) to Los Angeles daily; and flights from Australia (ex Sydney) to Toronto five times a week.

Air New Zealand has flights from New Zealand (ex Auckland) to Toronto four times a week.

Mexicana Airlines has flights from Australia (ex Melbourne and Sydney) to Mexico City daily.

Aerolineas Argentinas has flights from New Zealand (ex Auckland) to Buenos Aires twice a week.

By Sea

Although some visitors arrive by boat, its not really a serious option yet. Vessels can, however, enter Cuba via marinas at Havana, Varadero or Cayo Largo (these marinas can also help with visa applications). Each year dozens of yachting boffins from the USA defy their government and journey to the Marina Hemingway, just outside Havana, to take part in fishing competitions and boat races.

From November 1996, the Italian company *Costa Line* will bring a weekly cruise ship (capacity 450 people) to Havana, Santiago de Cuba and Nipe (Holguín Province).

Tours to Cuba

Travel agencies and organisations that arrange tours to Cuba include:

From Australia

Caribbean Destinations, Level 38, 525 Collins Street, Vic 3000, ph (03) 9621 2713.

Contours Travel, 1st Floor, 466 Victoria Street, North Melbourne Vic 3051, ph (03) 9329 5211.

Cubatours, 235 Swan Street, Richmond Vic 3121, ph (03) 9428 0385.

The Australia-Cuba Friendship Society, PO Box 1, 52 Victoria Street, Carlton South Vic 3053, ph (03) 9857 9249.

From the USA

Centre for Cuban Studies, 124 West 23rd Street, New York NY 10011, ph (212) 242 0559.

Marazul Tours, Suite 1311, 250 West 57th Street, New York NY 10107, ph (212) 582 9570.

From Canada

Alba Tours, 790 Arrom Road, Weston, Ontario, ph (416) 746 2890.

Canadian Holidays, 191 West Mall, Toronto, Ontario, ph (416) 620 8050.

Carousel Holidays, 125 Norfinch Drive, Downsview, Ontario M3N 1W8, ph (416) 665 7700.

Cuba Tourist Board, Suite 705, 55 Queen Street, Toronto, Ontario M5C 1R5, ph (416) 362 0700.

Magna Holidays, Suite 200C, 50 Alness Street, Downsview, Ontario M3J 2G9, ph (416) 665 7330.

Regent Holidays, Suite 300, Building A, 6205 Airport Road, Mississauga, Ontario L4V 1E1, ph (416) 673 0777.

From the UK

Aquatours, 7 Cranes Drive, Surbiton, Surrey, ph (0181) 339 9477.

Cosmos Holidays, Cosmosair, Tourma House, 17 Homesdale Road, Bromley, Kent BR2 94X, ph (0181) 464 3444.

Havanatur UK, 27 Stafford Road, Croydon, Surrey CRO 4NG, ph (0181) 681 3613.

Progressive Tours, 12 Porchester Place, Marble Arch, London W2 2BS, ph (0171) 262 1676.

Regent Holidays, 15 John Street, Bristol BS1 2HR, ph (0117) 921 1711.

South American Experience, 47 Causton Street, London SW1P 4AT, ph (0171) 976 5511.

Sunworld, 71 Hough Side Road, Pudsey, LS28 9BR, ph (0113) 2393020.

Voyages Jules Verne, 21 Dorset Square, London NW1 6QC, ph (0171) 723 4038.

From Venezuela

Ideal Tours, Centro Capriles, Olaza Venezuela, ph (010 582) 793 0037.

From Jamaica

UTAS Tours, PO Box 429, Montego Bay, ph (809) 979 0684.

Tourist Information

Cubatur, Cubanacán, Havanatur, Gaviota, Intur, Assistur and *Servitur* provide information, book tours and offer assistance to the traveller. Most have branches throughout the country (see individual chapters for more information). The larger hotels also have tourist offices that provide the same services.

Accommodation

The standard of accommodation has improved considerably in Cuba over the last few years as the government unabashedly goes after dollars. This is reflected in a range of top to middle-end lodgings that encompass everything from five-star hotels to villas, resorts, thatched-roof cabanas, former fortresses and mock castles. Unfortunately, there's not much bottom-end accommodation. To compensate, canny Cubans have opened their homes and rent out rooms for around $10-15 per day. They're almost always excellent deals and often include electric fan, TV, fridge, private bathroom and meals; enquire locally as they're not advertised. If you're persuasive, you might also be able to stay in a peso-only hotel, but at the time of writing, the government had made these establishments off-limits to foreigners. When staying in cheaper accommodation be prepared for Cuba's exiguous rationing: I would often wake to find no eggs on the menu, no soap in the bathroom, no running water from the taps, no electricity; sometimes it was overwhelming.

Check-out time across the island is a leisurely 2 pm.

Campismo Popular operate campsites in every province for around $5 per day (some charge in pesos). Often set in lovely surroundings, they have extensive facilities and can arrange a number of tours; contact Cubatur or the Palacio del Turismo in Havana for more information.

Prices covered in this book are low season (May to June and September to November) followed by high season (December to April and July to August) for single accommodation, unless stated otherwise. During high season it is advisable to book accommodation in advance (especially in Havana and Santiago de Cuba).

Local Transport

Air

Cubana flies to major destinations such as Varadero, Santiago de Cuba, Holguín, Cienfuegos, and Camagüey as well as Isla de la Juventud and Cayo Largo. Tickets should be purchased well in advance from Cubana offices (be prepared to wait; they're always busy) and paid for in dollars.

Aerocaribbean Aerogaviota also fly to destinations throughout Cuba.

Rail

Train travel is cheap and reasonably comfortable but the pace is hardly electrifying. Expect long waits at stations, delays caused by heavy rains washing out tracks, and the inevitable breakdown. Also, don't rely on overhead announcements to tell you of your arrival - it rarely comes, and if it does, it sounds like the person at the microphone has a mouthful of wet toilet paper. Train travel does, however, provide an opportunity to parley with Cubans and their happiness and good humour - often under trying circumstances - is infectious.

From Havana, trains run to a number of destinations including Pinar del Río (one way, three times a week, $6.50), Cienfuegos (three times a week, $11), Camagüey (daily, $22), Las Tunas (daily, $26), Bayamo (daily, $27) and Santiago de Cuba (three times a week, $35). Tickets can be purchased in dollars from Ferrotur offices at the railway stations. Remember to bring water bottles and pesos to pay for the stale bread rolls that are intermittently doled out on the longer journeys.

NOTES

Bus

Luxurious air-con buses (usually taking tour groups) regularly run from Havana to major destinations such as Varadero and Santiago de Cuba; journeys can be booked at large hotels or tourist agencies. Small and very rare buses also run between Havana and the larger cities. They're cramped and stuffy and getting a ticket (pesos only) is often a shorthand for confusion: long queues; booking offices are shut; buses sometimes don't run, etc.

Buying a Bus Ticket

In Cuba the demand for bus tickets often exceeds the supply of seats. However, don't fret - there's a number of options open to you. These include:

*making sure you buy a ticket well in advance.

*going to the bus station (when seats are unavailable) around 6-7am and asking for 'missing' seats (*la lista de fatta*); these, in effect, are available seats at a later date which should then be registered in your name.

*buying tickets on the black market by going to the bus station (again, as early as possible) and waiting in the queue; a Cuban will almost always approach you to buy the ticket in your name for a small fee.

*persuading the driver of an already full bus to let you on (standing room only) by offering to pay a slightly higher fare.

Car

Even though its expensive, travelling by car is far and away the best means of seeing Cuba. The roads vary from good (Havana, Santiago de Cuba, the Pinar del Río-Havana-Santa Clara expressway) to truly awful (most roads in rural areas are a mess of potholes and obstinate farm animals).

Cars can be rented from a number of companies including *Havanautos* and *Cubacar*. Prices range from $45 per day (for a Nissan Sunny LX) to $130 (for a Mercedes Benz 190E) with discount rates for weekly hire. The first 100km are free; after that you'll be stung another $0.30 for each additional kilometre. Expect to pay a further $8 per day for insurance. Dune buggies and open-top jeeps are also available at Varadero and other beach resorts for $30-50 per day.

An international drivers licence or a valid drivers licence from your country of origin is necessary to rent a car. Payment is in dollars or by credit card and a deposit of $100 is sometimes required. The maximum speed limit is 50 km/h in urban areas and 100 km/h on the open roads. Driving is on the right.

Petrol is supplied at special tourist stations but is limited outside Havana (make sure you get the addresses of petrol stations that serve foreigners from your rental company). If you're driving long distances, take an extra can of petrol with you. The cost of filling an empty tank is around $70.

Taxi

Turistaxi, *Cubanacán*, *Panataxis* and *Gaviota* all operate taxi services for foreigners. Reservations can be made at hotels or by telephone for pick-up service. Payment is made to the driver in dollars only. Most of the newer taxis are metered and there is often a call-out charge. Cubans will often carry foreigners in private cars; they're usually cheaper than official taxis, but agree on a fee beforehand.

Hitching

Hitching is almost a way of life for many Cubans. Chronic petrol shortages and a lack of spare parts has resulted in a number of working planes, trains, buses and cars now sitting idle. Purchasing tickets for peso transport is also fraught with difficulties. It's common then to see hordes of people hitching within and to/from cities (especially in Havana, where people alight from one vehicle and then promptly get into another, and along the Vía Blanca, a sealed highway that links East Havana to Varadero) or to some of the places off the beaten track. In some areas in Cuba, motorists are obliged to pick up hitchers.

If you do decide to hitch you should realise that there exists a small but potentially serious risk. If possible, tell someone where you're going. And if you don't speak Spanish, take a sign clearly showing your destination. In addition, bring along a hat to protect you from the sun; waits for rides can be tediously long. Rides are usually free, though you should offer to pay or give a gift.

Food

There's an attempt to bridge the gulf between Cuban cuisine and the food served in Cuba with socialist rhetoric and tourist brochure propaganda, but after a few days in the country you're unlikely to swallow it. Although the Revolution undoubtedly improved the diet of the majority of the population, Cuba's inefficient, centralised, agricultural policy is now handicapping food production and distribution. During the first public anti-Castro riots in Havana on 5 August 1994, the crowd began shouting for freedom but ended chanting *'Comida!'* ('Food!')!

There is hunger in Cuba today, despite the island's fertility and its potential to produce adequate food supplies. The US embargo has caused disastrous shortages of seeds, fertilisers and farm machinery. Since 1961, shortages have required more and more staple ingredients to be rationed - hardly a prerequisite for the development of a dynamic national cuisine.

So when you're queuing at a restaurant, struggling to find a store that has anything on its shelves, or chewing on unpalatable gristle for the third day in a row, remember that as a traveller with US dollars, you are still sheltered from many of the hardships of obtaining food. Foreigners queue-jumping at eateries, and the existence of dollar stores and restaurants are part of the apartheid of eating that has developed in Cuba today.

Another development is the advent of *paladares* (living-room restaurants that serve food to foreigners). They're a great opportunity to see how Cubans live and the food is cheap; for around $5 you get mammoth portions of beans, rice, chicken, salad, refreshments, etc. Don't be surprised when your hosts leave the room once the meal has been served - they simply don't want to disturb you while you eat.

Despite all this, travellers should be prepared to lose weight, eat disgusting food, be haunted by strange gastronomic longings, and to gorge maniacally on anything fresh you find for sale.

Cuban Cuisine

Cuba's creole cuisine is based on indigenous foods, and a marriage of Spanish and African influences. This has been overlaid in recent years by imported fads for US junk, and canned and processed food.

The Amerindians grew cassava, corn and squash; African slaves brought yams, okra and plantains; and the Spanish introduced rice, beans and tomatoes. These staples are combined with local fish, pork, chicken and beef in colourful dishes seasoned with saffron, paprika, cumin and oregano.

The most prevalent local dishes are: *Moros y Cristianos* or Moors and Christians (rice with black beans); *arroz con pollo* (chicken and rice); *picadillo* (minced beef and rice); *ajiaco* (a peasant stew made of just about every available root vegetable and various meats); and plaintain, chick-pea and bean soups.

Many meat dishes are cooked in a blend of onions, tomatoes, capsicums, garlic and herbs known as *sofrita*. These dishes are usually prepared with a cavalier disregard for measurements, ingredients and timing, but with a great feel for taste and innovation. The food is spicy and well-seasoned rather than hot.

You could be forgiven for thinking that Cuban desserts have been

---

A Taste of Paradise

The three year war of attrition which began in 1895 not only led to Cuba's independence, it also introduced desiccated coconut to the US market. Disruption to the Cuban economy resulted in a local entrepreneur having to repay his debt to a Philadelphian flour miller in the form of coconuts. The US businessman's schemes to sell the cargo of coconuts were inventive but fruitless; that is, until he struck on the idea of shredding and drying the coconut meat and selling it to bakers and confectioners.

The desperate stop-gap idea, forced on the businessman by circumstance, proved so successful that he eventually built a processing plant expressly for the production of desiccated coconut.

Where would the Bounty bar be without José Martí?

---

specifically designed to use up as much of the sugar crop as possible. *Natilla* (sweet custard), *cururucho* (coconut and cocoa wrapped in banana leaves), *leche frita* (fried squares of milk), *boniatillo* (sweet potato paste), and *coco quemado* (coconut crisp) are partially responsible for some less-than-athletic physiques. Cuba is also renowned for its ice cream, which takes full advantage of local fruits, but be prepared to wait in line for a scoop.

Fruits

Cuba has a large citrus-growing industry, but much of the produce is exported as juice. Oranges, lemons and limes are all grown in large-scale citrus groves. Other delicious tropical fruits include mango, guava, papaya, passion fruit, pineapple, melon, banana, avocado, grapefruit and coconut. More exotic fruits include custard apple, the sweet zapote, and the prickly guanabana. If you find any of these fruits being sold at roadside stalls, reintroduce your body to vitamin C.

Drinks

Non-Alcoholic Drinks

Coffee

Cubans drink vast quantities of strong, ultrasweet, viscous espresso-style coffee served in tiny cups, which may account for their high rate of heart attacks. Coffee is drunk black, except at breakfast, when it is topped with a foam of milk. White coffee at any other time of the day is the reserve of small children. Small, standing-only cafés selling cups of coffee (pesos only) can be found throughout the country.

Fruit and Soft Drinks

Cuba has a large variety of fruit drinks, usually based around orange, lemon, lime, pineapple, grapefruit or guava. *Batidos* are pretty good, but the more common *Refresco* is a diluted version tasting of 99% sugar and 1% fruit. If you don't like bits of fruit getting in the way of your sugar hit, try the freshly pressed *guarapo* (sugar cane juice).

African influences can be seen in the use of tamarind and baobab pods which are added to sugar and water to produce drinks. The imperialist colas are banned, but the local *Tropicola* is a palatable alternative. *Malta*, a drink made of sugar, caramel, hops and water is also popular. Coconut milk is the only type of milk that is safe to drink - distribution and refrigeration problems mean most milk is of unreliable quality.

Alcoholic Drinks

Beer

Cubans used to drink more beer (*cerveza*) than rum, but in urban areas beer is now in short supply and may only be bought with dollars. The fact that Cubans sometimes perversely mix their beer with tomato juice should not cause too much consternation; if you feel strongly about this but still have a strong thirst, there's plenty of rum available as an alternative.

One of the strongest local beers is *Hatuey* (named after the Indian chief who fought the Spaniards), although most travellers prefer the tasty *Tropical Negra*. Other brands include *Bucanero, Cristal, Lobo, Manacas* and *Polar*. Imported European and US beers are available in hotels, restaurants and dollar stores. Beer is usually served cold in bottles, but in the country it may be dispensed in voluminous paper cups.

Imported Wines and Spirits

High-quality Russian Vodka (*Stolichnaya*) used to be widely available and certainly broadened the possibilities of cocktail recipes, but the collapse of the USSR and Cuba's favourable trade agreements with the Eastern bloc has curtailed supplies. The good news is that thanks to the lack of taxes, Scotch whisky is still available cheaper than it is in the UK. Some imported wines from South America are of acceptable quality; Bulgarian and Romanian wines are the comic by-products of trade alliances forced on Cuba by circumstance. You may find other dinosaurs of these trade agreements, in the form of Armenian brandy,

Lithuanian port and Estonian champagne.

Cocktails

While the USA was suffering under Prohibition, Havana was the cocktail centre of the world. Famous Cuban cocktails like the *mojito*, *daiquiri* and *Cuba libre* are now drunk throughout the world, but their histories are evocatively caught up in a time when Havana was a swinging town and bars like

> ## Recipe for a Good Time
>
> **To make the perfect *Mojito* you need 30ml of Havana Club silver dry Cuban rum, half a teaspoon of sugar, a few mint leaves, some lemon juice, ice cubes and soda water. Mix the ingredients together, stir or shake (whatever's your preference) and voilá - a crisp, refreshing drink that makes an ideal accompaniment to an aromatic Cohiba cigar.**

Sloppy Joe's and *La Floridita* were regarded as the best in the world.

Nearly all of the famous Cuban cocktails are a blend of rum, sugar and local fruits. The *daiquiri* is a blend of light rum, sugar and lime poured onto crushed ice. The *mojito* is similar, but includes a sprig of fresh mint (often unavailable in Cuba; carry your own supplies!) and a dash of Angostura bitters. Hemingway invented his own version which replaced the sugar with grapefruit juice and a dash of maraschino liqueur. The *Cuba libre* is concocted from light rum and lemon juice poured onto crushed ice and lemon peel and topped up with cola. *Saoco* is a rum and coconut mix, unfortunately usually served in a cumbersome coconut shell.

Canchánchara, a delicious blend of *aguardiente* (raw rum), honey, lemon and water, is one of the oldest cocktails in Cuba. Believed to be the forerunner of the *daiquiri*, it was the beverage of choice among the *mambíses* (Cuban soldiers who fought in the wars of independence). The *canchánchara* is also thought to have heady curative powers but unfortunately its not easily found in Cuban bars. There is, however, a bar in Trinidad specialising in it and Apisun cafés often have plentiful stock.

Other Cuban rum cocktail standards include: *Cubanito* (similar to a Bloody Mary but hold the vodka and use Light Dry rum); *Presidente* (Light Dry rum, red Curaçao, Amat or Chamberry Vermouth, a twist of orange peel and a cherry); and *Cuba Bella* (Light Dry rum, Extra Aged Dry rum, crème de menthe, grenadine, lemon juice and ice).

You should think twice about trying the local firewater. Commonly known as *chispa del tren* ('train spark'), its a sure-fire way to induce vomiting and worse.

The Genesis of the Daiquiri

There are many apocryphal stories about the invention and naming of the *daiquiri*, from the prosaic to the mythological. Some claim it was named after the town of Daiquirí in south-eastern Cuba, where a US mining engineer invented the drink in 1896. A more colourful version recounts the story of a nameless young black man who entered *La Floridita* bearing his own bottle of rum and casually concocted the drink to thank the patrons for encouraging the management to let him stay. According to this legend, the drink became popular but remained without a name until the old black newspaper seller who sat outside the bar was asked by a patron one night if the drink was available inside. He replied '*Ah, da kirie*' ('Yes, sir') - in the linguistic confusion, the cocktail got it's name.

Entertainment

Cinema

There are cinemas in all major cities and towns. Most screen old Mexican melodramas, fifth-rate Hollywood action flics, or Hong Kong-made martial arts epics. For some reason, they all attract *huge* audiences. Probably the only chance you'll get of seeing first-run movies will be at selected cinemas in Havana or by attending that city's Latin American Film Festival (December).

Admission to Cuban movies is cheap at around one or two pesos, but away from Havana the experience can often be frustrating: film and sound quality can be patchy; and there's always the threat of a power blackout.

Bars, Cafés and Nightclubs

Major tourist destinations such as Havana and Varadero have an ample choice of things to do after dark - from cabarets and bars, to cafés, nightclubs and meat-market discos. There's also a flourishing live music scene in Havana. While not as varied (or raucous), the nightlife in the remainder of the country does have its moments, with the *Casa de la Trova* in Santiago de Cuba, immediately springing to mind.

Theatre

Theatres scattered throughout the country present ballet, song and dance spectaculars, opera, and classical music. For many, the highlight of any visit to the theatre is the setting - usually in some white-marble mansion from bygone times. Performances are common most evenings, with matinees on weekends. Tickets for the more popular shows can be purchased from the box office or from major hotels; prices will, of course, depend entirely on where you choose to sit. Payment is in dollars.

Shopping

Cuba is hardly a shopper's paradise. But with time, patience and a fair amount of luck, you can find good *haute couture* evening wear from Dior to Versace (try *La Maison* in Havana and Santiago de Cuba), sportswear, and major brands of electronic goods, footwear, jewellery, cigars and rum. For men, the *guayabera* (a light Cuban shirt that is not tucked in) is an inexpensive reminder of your stay, while cassettes and CDs of Cuban music are also cheap and readily available.

The cult of Ché Guevara, and the ardour that surrounds him, is pervasive in Cuba. He may be dead but he's still doing his economic bit for the Revolution: his unkempt mien adorns T-shirts, postcards, posters, buttons and pins, all of which can be bought from dollar stores, street stalls and tourist hotels. Cuban craftsmanship is generally good and most wood, leather, coconut, ceramic and *yarey* (the leaf of the fan palm) products are sold at reasonable prices. Avoid, if you can, the tourist bric-a-brac that line the sidewalks outside most major hotels - forlorn collections of combs, nail clippers and key rings made of Kodak film canisters. Awful!

Sports

Sport was rarely promoted by Cuban governments prior to the Revolution. However all that changed in 1961 with the founding of the National Institute for Sports, Physical Education and Recreation (INDER). Sporting activities were encouraged throughout the country, professionalism stamped out - prompting some Cuban athletes, especially baseball players, to relocate to the USA - and the public given free admission to most major events.

Since then, Cuba has become one of the worlds leading sporting powers. The country has hosted a number of international events (for instance, the 1991 Pan American Games), and produced some of the finest athletic talent in the last twenty years including Alberto Juantorena, the Olympic 400 and 800-metre champion; Teofilo Stevenson, the three-time Olympic and world super-heavyweight boxing champion; and Marisa Marten, the Olympic discus champion.

Cuba can also boast two men who have jumped higher and further than anyone in history - Javier Sotomayor, the Olympic high-jump champion, and Ivan Pedroso, who, on July 29, 1995, broke the world long jump record with a leap of 8.96 metres. (Unfortunately for Pedroso, an administrative quirk - an official was found standing in front of the wind meter - robbed him of the record less than a week later.) Cuba's latest sporting success is Ana Quirot, Castro's favourite athlete, who won gold in the 800 metres at the 1995 World Athletics Championship in Gothenburg.

Fishing

Cuba has excellent opportunities for fishing (especially between December and May) with wahoo, striped tuna, red schnapper, jurels, barracuda, sawfish and marlin readily found off its coast. The headquarters for marlin fishing is the Marina Hemingway, near Havana.

For largemouth bass, the best fishing is at Lake Hanabanilla, Zaza Reservoir, Laguna Redonda, Laguna de la Leche and Laguna del Tesoro.

Scuba Diving

Cuba is second only to Australia for having the largest coral barrier in the world, and now attracts thousands of scuba divers each year. Diving is excellent along Cuba's northern and southern coasts, with more than 700 sq km of island platform. North coast dive spots include Havana, Playas del Este and Varadero, which have cliffs, caverns, sunken ships, tubular sponges, wire corals and many species of fish. South coast dive spots number Cayo Largo, Isla de la Juventud, Cienfuegos and Trinidad.

Baseball

Baseball is the national sport and the country's prowess is such that it has held world, Pan-American, Central American and Olympic titles.

Soccer

The sport of soccer is gradually gaining a toe-hold in Cuba, thanks to the national team's recent success in Caribbean tournaments. However the players still lack the élan and technical skill of their Latin American counterparts (the national soccer body would be wise to seek out Argentina's Diego Maradona who holidays in Cuba - often staying at Castro's home - for some assistance).

Other Sports

Water sports such as jet skiing, windsurfing and beach volleyball are popular in the resort areas, and facilities for golf and tennis are available (if limited). A new golf course is being built in Varadero and others are planned for Havana, Santa Lucía (Camagüey Province), Guardalavaca (Holguín Province) and Siboney (Santiago de Cuba Province).

Soccer, Havana style.

HAVANA

Confusion surrounds the date of Havana's founding - archives mysteriously went missing in a pirate raid - but it is thought to be in 1514. The first settlement, called San Cristóbal de la Habana, was on Cuba's south-west coast but was moved twice because of unsanitary conditions. Finally, in 1519, it came to occupy the position it now has on the country's northern coast.

Within a few years, the settlement had flourished. Havana became a port of passage for Spanish exploration to the New World, and a compulsory way-station for merchant ships, their holds laden with alpaca, wood, silver and gold. In 1538 mercantile peace was shattered when French corsairs - aided and abetted by African slaves - stormed and set Havana alight. Although the authorities attempted to fortify the city, its coastal defences remained weak, and the pickings rich.

Havana grew despite the constant menace of attack, and by 1553 it was the largest and most important city on the island. Five years later it was declared the nation's capital.

Over the years, Havana's fortunes rose and fell. The city was captured and occupied by the English in 1762 but profited enormously when they lifted trading restrictions, allowing it to become a free port. (It was during this time that Havana was described as the 'boulevard of the New World and one of the gayest and most picturesque ports on the shores of equinoctial America'.) The city's economy boomed in the sugar-rich years of the mid-18th century, only to bottom out when slavery was abolished. By 1920, another recovery: an influx of US capital coupled with soaring sugar prices sparked the so-called 'dance of millions' - a period of short-lived prosperity that saw the building of sumptuous mansions, hotels and casinos. Havana became a playground capital, a Latin American facsimile of urban USA.

Soon after, a string of brutish and dictatorial leaders - including Fulgencio Batista who amassed a fortune along the way - came and went. Public office was viewed with widespread disdain. The city, fed on rumours and charges of corruption, political favours and misappropriation, took on an increasingly violent character. When Castro and his rebels entered Havana in 1959, they were greeted by enormous crowds baying for change.

Havana, under Castro, did change - and how. Homosexuals were press-ganged into *sidatorios* (sanatoriums), prostitutes were yanked from the streets, foreigners discourteously sent packing, and hotels and casinos closed. Formless, Soviet-style apartments sprung up - 'reward for the revolutionary faithful' - and fortresses were turned into schools. The government's thrust to develop the countryside also meant that many of Havana's magnificent buildings, including those in its colonial core, were neglected. For Ché Guevara, whose loathing of the city was legendary, Havana was grist to the revolutionary treadmill - a 'Yanquí' collaborationist to be condemned.

Today Havana (population 2,200,000) is a city yet in its ascendancy. Its buildings still suffer from decades of neglect with over half of all dwellings considered in a 'regular' or poor state. Yet however hard the 'blows of revolutionary justice', Havana remains a revelation for the first-time visitor: the rough brilliance of Old Havana with its tree-filled plazas and chatty, elegant streets; swimmers, their slick bodies glistening under a canopy of the bluest sky, lounge along the walls of the Malecón - a weekend ritual; the Prado, laurel-lined and lit by wrought-iron lamp posts; cyclists competing with rusting flotillas of corpulent Chevys and Cadillacs; fishermen lugging inner tubes; shirtless teenagers playing basketball; and salsa blaring from open doorways.

Its mix of peoples - from Spanish to Jamaican, Jew to Chinese - al fresco cafés, hotels, resorts, and nightlife testify to Havana's metropolitan accent. And while former writer-in-residence Ernest Hemingway is long dead, there's another man in town more than capable of filling his shoes - Gabriel García Márquez, the celebrated novelist, who now lives in Havana for six months of the year.

How to get there

By Air

For information on how to get to Havana see the Travel Information chapter. Facilities at the twin terminals (a taxi between them is around $3) of the José Martí International Airport are basic but you can arrange accommodation, hire rental cars, change money and purchase duty-free goods, city guides, maps and postcards. The Aerocaribbean terminal is just west of the José Martí International Airport, about 3km away.

A taxi from the airport to the city (about a 20-minute drive) is officially $14 but private cars will take you there for $10.

The following airline offices are in Havana:

Aerocaribbean, Calle 23 e/ Infanta y P, Vedado, ph 79 7525.
Aeroflot, Calle 23 e/ Infanta y P, Vedado, ph 33 3200.
Air Canada, José Martí International Airport, ph 33 5257.
Cubana, Calle 23 e/ Infanta y P, Vedado, ph 33 4949.
Mexicana Airlines, Calle 23 e/ Infanta y P, Vedado, ph 33 3730.

Tourist Information

Tourist offices include:

Cubanacán, Calle 136, e/ 11 y 13, Playa, ph 21 6936.
Cubatur, Calle 23, No 156, Vedado, ph 32 4521.
Gaviota, Calle 16 e/ 5 y 7, Miramar, ph 22 1059.
Havanatur, Calle 2, No 17, Miramar, ph 33 2121.

The *Palacio de Turismo*, cnr calles OReilly and Bernaza, Old Havana, can arrange tours, while *Asistur*, Prado No 254, Old Havana, ph 62 5519, helps travellers with financial, legal and medical emergencies, and can make reservations for accommodation, entertainment and transport. If your belongings have been lost or stolen, no sweat - they're the people to see. Most of the major hotels have a travel desk or booking agency.

The *Banco Financiero International*, Calle Línea No 1, Vedado, ph 33 3423, changes travellers cheques and provides business services for foreigners.

Postal services exist in all the major hotels and there is a branch of *Cubapost* at Calle Obispo No 518, Old Havana. Photoservice branches are on the corner of calles 23 and O and immediately behind the Habana Libre Hotel, both in Vedado, and on Calle Obispo, Old Havana.

Accommodation

Vedado

Meliá Cohiba, Paseo y Calle 1ra, ph 33 3636 - 462 rooms, Cuba's premier hotel, very modern, enormous shrub-filled lobby, full range of business services, gym, bars, nightclub, good shops, pool - $140-170.

Nacional de Cuba, cnr calles O and 21, ph 33 3564 - 495 rooms, superb seaworn old hotel and *the* place to stay in Havana, formerly the haunt of mobsters and international politicians, marvellous location overlooking the bay with the city at its feet, olde-worlde furnishings, attentive staff, business services, pharmacy, nightclub and cabaret, excellent dining room, two pools - $125-155.

Habana Libre, Calle L e/ 23 y 25, ph 33 3704 - 606 rooms, towering edifice (badly in need of a face-lift) that was once the Havana Hilton and meeting place for Castro and his chums, the current Mecca for foreigners in Havana, excellent location - right on the corner of 'La Rampa', Vedado's humming agora - with good views, close to airline offices and the city's best cinemas, good shops (reasonably current issues of *Time* and *Newsweek* on sale), business and congress facilities, extensive tour services, nightclub, better than average handicrafts sold in the street below, pool - $70-90.

Victoria, cnr calles 19 and M, ph 32 6531 - 34 rooms, business services, good food, very clean, pool - $65-79.

Riviera, Paseo y Malecón, ph 33 4051 - 382 rooms, splashy exterior, Jewish mobster Meyer Lansky blew a bundle on its construction - it was supposed to be his crowning achievement - when Castro nationalised foreign-owned businesses in 1960. Check out the decor (straight out of Holiday Inn) and the nightly lines of ditsy *jiniteras* waiting to get in, untrammelled views of the ocean, popular nightclub, saltwater pool - $60-$75.

Presidente, Calle Calzada e/ F y G, ph 32 7521 - 144 rooms, quiet setting, furnished with 1930s curios, good food and service, pool - $47-60.

Capri, Calle 21 e / N y O, ph 32 0511 - 235 rooms, nightclub, nice downstairs bar, popular with American tourists, pool - $45-56.

Vedado, Calle O e/ 23 y 25, ph 32 6501 - 191 rooms, good location, nightclub, pool - $40-53.

St Johns, Calle O e/ 23 y 25, ph 32 9531 - 94 rooms, nightclub, pool - $32-45.

Colina, Calle L e/ 27 y Jovellar, ph 32 3535 - 84 rooms, student hangout, close to the University of Havana, tiny rooms, drab - $30-40.

Morro, Calle 3ra e/ D y C, ph 32 5907 - 24 rooms - $30-40.

Old Havana

Sevilla, Calle Trocadero No 55, ph 33 8560 - good café, the best hotel in Old Havana, setting for Graham Greene's *Our Man in Havana*, great location, lovely interior furnishings, shops, restaurant, sun-filled café, very friendly tour agency, nightclub, pool - $70-90.

Plaza, Calle Ignacio Agramonte No 267, ph 33 8583 - 206 rooms, excellent location, very friendly downstairs café, solarium - $55-70.

Inglaterra, cnr calles Prado and San Rafael, ph 33 8593 - 86 rooms, oldest existing hotel in the city and declared a national monument, art nouveau exterior, good location, excellent food, expensive tourist shop, lacklustre travel agency, popular nightclub - $50-70.

Hostal Valencia, Calle Oficios e/ Lamparilla y Obrapía, ph 62 3801 - small 18th-century colonial palace-cum-hotel, charming atmosphere, abundance of tropical plants and wooden railing, good Spanish restaurant, very popular - $25-35.

Ambos Mundos, cnr calles Obispo and Mercaderes - Hemingway once stayed here, closed for renovation at the time of writing.

Caribbean, Prado No 164 e/ Colón y Refugio, ph 62 2071 - 36 rooms, central location, close to the city's best museums and historical sites, 20-minute walk from Vedado, budget travellers favourite and still the cheapest hotel in Havana though plans to renovate will increase prices, friendly staff, very popular downstairs restaurant and bar, some reports of theft from the rooms - $20-23.

For rental rooms in Old Havana, contact Evelito O Kenia, Apt A, Calle Virtudes No 312 e/ Galiano y San Nicolás, ph 61 3086 and Ivan Galarraya, Apt 303, Calle Empedradro No 360 e/ Habana y Compostela for more information.

Central Havana

Deauville, cnr calles Galiano and Malecón, ph 33 8812 - 142 rooms, excellent location on the Malecón with great views over the ocean, noisy downstairs bar, could do with a paint job, pool - $30-40.

Lincoln, Calle Galiano e/ Virtudes y Animas, ph 62 8061 - 145 rooms, reasonable facilities - $30-40.

Lido, Calle Consulado No 210 e/ Animas y Trocadero - cheap alternative to the Caribbean, closed for renovation at the time of writing.

Miramar

Comodoro, cnr calles 3ra and 84, ph 33 2011 - 139 rooms, comfortable bungalows, pool - $50-70.

Neptuno-Tritón, cnr calles 3 and 70, ph 33 1606 - 556 rooms, twin buildings, close to the beach, tennis courts, pool - $45-70.

Copacabana, Calle 1ra e/ 44 y 46, ph 33 1037 - 168 rooms, resort-style hotel, dreary Brazilian-tinged atmosphere, pool - $40-70.

Marina Hemingway

El Viejo y el Mar ('The Old Man and the Sea'), Santa Fe, ph 68822 - 146 rooms, lots of facilities, the domain of package tourists and yachting/fishing afficianados from the USA - $123-145.

Cerro

Bruzón, Calle Bruzón e/ Pozos Dulces y Boyeros, Cerro, ph 70 3531 - 48 rooms, near the Plaza de la Revolución and bus station, noisy but cheap - $18-23.

East Havana Beaches

Panamericano, Calle A y Ave Central, Cojímar, ph 68 4111 - 103 rooms, excellent gym, stress and weight treatments, good massages, body therapies, close proximity to important sports facilities, pool - $50-80.

Itabo, Laguna Itabo, Boca Siega, Santa María del Mar, Playa del Este, ph 2581 - 204 rooms, close to beach and surrounded by a lagoon, good pool - $38-50.

Atlántico, Ave de Las Terrazas, Santa María del Mar, Playa del Este, ph 2560 - 20 rooms, both hotel and apartment-style accommodation, barbecue, very popular, nightclub, pool - $22-30.

Vila Tropicoco, Arroyo Bermejo, Santa Cruz del Norte, Playa del Este, ph 83555 - 146 rooms, bungalow-style accommodation, close to the beach, nightclub, pool - $18-30.

Vila Playa Hermosa, 5ta Ave e/ 472 y 474, Playa del Este, ph 2774 - 33 rooms, pool, bike rental - $18-23.

Camping de Jibacoa, Jibacoa - two and four-bedded cabins - $12.

Local Transport

Rail

Havana's main railway station is on Calle Egido, south of Old Havana. Tickets can be purchased at the friendly and very helpful Ferrotur office behind the station, and at selected hotels such as the Habana Libre. Trains to Pinar del Río leave from the Estacion 19 de Noviembre, near the Plaza de la Revolución. The railway station at Casablanca (reached by ferry; see under **Boat,** following) is the departure point - via the Hershey Railway, Cuba's only electric train - for the scenic trip to Mantanzas City. Tickets should be bought from the Casablanca station well in advance.

Bus

Buses or *guaguas* (pronounced 'wa-was' and sometimes euphemistically called 'rolling units' because of their blimp-like size) are ridiculously cheap, but long waits and the sardine-like conditions inside mean they're often not worth the hassle. Ciclo buses (hollowed-out buses used to transport Havana's legion of cyclists) are much better value and travel under the harbour from Old Havana to East Havana for 10-40 centavos. Take one from Ave de los Estudiantes, near the Máximo Gómez statue, for the Castillo del Morro.

The main bus station is on Ave Rancho Boyeros, south of Vedado.

Taxi

There are taxi stands outside most hotels. Turistaxis are among the cheapest operators and charge around $4 between Old Havana and Vedado. If you take any one of the myriad private cars used as taxis, agree on a fare beforehand. Service can be requested by calling the following: Cubalse, ph 33 6558; Cubanacán, ph 33 1446; Gaviota, ph 23 7000; Panataxi, ph 81 0153; Turistaxi, ph 33 5539; Veracuba, ph 33 1890.

Car

Vehicles can be rented at the José Martí International Airport and larger hotels. Car rental companies include: Cubacar, ph 20 2188; Cubalse, ph 33 6558; Gaviota, ph 23 7000; Havanautos, ph 33 2369; Transautos, ph 33 5532.

Petrol can be bought from the following service stations (open every day):

El Motor, 5ta Ave y 112, Miramar.

L y 17, cnr calles L and 17, Vedado.

Servicentre Cubalse, Calle 2 No 518, Miramar.

Servicupet, Ave 18 y 31, Miramar.

Servi Riviera, Paseo y Malecón, Vedado.

Tángana, Malecón y 11, Vedado.

Bicycle

Bicycles can be rented from Panaciclos, ph 81 0153, for $1 an hour. Some hotels such as the Riviera, and tourist agencies, also rent bikes for around $12 a day.

Boat

Irregular ferries run from Old Havana (there are docks east of El Castillo de la Real Fuerza and at the eastern end of Calle Santa Clara) across Havana Bay to the towns of Casablanca and Regla for 50 centavos.

Malecón, Havana.

Eating Out

Havana's licensed eateries are many and varied but they are fairly expensive. Prices range from $10-30 for a standard meal but they can be much steeper when drinks are included. Some of the city's establishments are also notorious for overcharging; when paying, make sure that the bill tallies with what you ate and drank.

The major hotels such as the Habana Libre, Nacional de Cuba, Inglaterra and Sevilla have a number of cafés and restaurants that are good value, but vegetarians and the budget-conscious will find the unavailability of menu items and the lack of variety (rice, omelettes, spaghetti and cheese sandwiches seem to be staples) exasperating. There are, however, other options including the widely-advertised *oferta especial* (a voucher which gives travellers a hefty discount on buffets in the larger hotels), supermarkets, a few produce markets and many excellent *paladares*; enquire locally for their location.

Payment for the following is in dollars or by credit card (unless stated otherwise).

International

Vedado

Club 23, Calle 23 e/ N y O, ph 32 9350 - open every day noon-midnight.

Emperador, Calle 17 e/ M y N, ph 32 4998 - open every day noon-midnight - very popular.

Las Bulerías, Calle L e/ 23 y 25, ph 32 3283 - open every day 10am-6pm.

Monseigneur, cnr calles O and 21, ph 32 9884 - open every day noon-midnight.

Restaurante 1830, Malecón No 1252, ph 34504 - open every day
 noon-midnight - good food and excellent location near waterfront.

Restaurante La Torre, Calle 17 No 55 e/ M y N, ph 32 5650 - open every day noon-11pm.

Old Havana

El Patio, cnr calles San Ignacio and Empedrado, ph 65 8504 - open every day noon-11pm - good location, very expensive.

El Patio Colonial, cnr calles Baratillo and Obispo, ph 33 4186 - open every day 10am-midnight - expensive.

La Piña de Plata, cnr calles Obispo and Bernaza, ph 63 1063 - open every day 10am-11pm.

Miramar

Casa de 5ta y 16, cnr 5ta Ave and Calle 16, ph 29 4040 - open Mon-Sat noon-10.30pm.

El Tocororo, cnr calles 18 and 3ra, ph 33 4530 - open every day noon-11pm - located in old mansion, big favourite with diplomats and business people, superb grilled meat dishes, very pricey.

La Cecilia, Calle 5ta Ave e/ 110 y 112, ph 33 1562 - open every day noon-midnight - pleasant surroundings, toffy service.

La Ferminia, 5ta Ave No 18207, ph 33 6555 - open every day - noon-11pm - excellent wine list.

La Fuente, cnr 5ta Ave and Calle 42, ph 33 2372 - open every day noon-10pm.

Cuban

El Ranchón, Ave 19 y Calle 140, Miramar, ph 33 1984 - open every day 10am-10pm - superb food.

La Bodeguita del Medio, Calle Empedrado No 207, Old Havana, ph 62 4498 - open every day 11.30am-1am - small and cosy hole-in-the-wall, covered inside with inscriptions, signatures and overly enthusiastic allusions to the food, crusty old Hemingway used to come here to quaff *mojitos* (this is where they were supposedly invented), pseudo-bohemian atmosphere that is the haunt of politicians, painters, writers and wannabees, lots of elbow grease is required to get past the package tourists at the door, good roof terrace, live Cuban music a feature at night.

Las Ruinas, Calle Cortina de la Presa y Carretera del Globo, South Havana, ph 44 3336 - open Tue-Sun noon-midnight - sober and elegant colonial atmosphere built around the ruins of an old sugar mill, exclusive and very expensive.

Los 12 Apóstoles, Castillo del Morro, East Havana, ph 63 8295 - noon-midnight - excellent location with great views but nondescript food.

Italian

D'Giovanni, cnr calles Tacón No 4 and Empedrado, Old Havana, ph 61 2183 - open every day, 11am-11pm - nice views, also offers Cuban and international cuisine.

La Cova, Marina Hemingway, Calle 248 y 5ta, Playa, ph 33 1150 - open every day 7am-1am - good pasta and pizza, home delivery.

La Torre del Mangia, 5ta Ave e/ 40 y 42, Miramar, ph 33 2450 - open every day 7.30am-8.30pm.

Spanish

Fiesta, Marina Hemingway, Calle 248 y 5ta, Playa, ph 33 1150 - open every day noon-2am.

La Paella, Calle Oficios e/ Lamparilla y Obrapía, Old Havana, ph 62 3801 - open every day 6.30am-8.30pm.

Meson la Chorrera, cnr Malecón No 1252 and Calle 20, Vedado, ph 34504 - open every day 6pm-midnight.

Chinese

El Mandarín, cnr calles 23 and M, Vedado, ph 32 0677 - open Fri-Sun 6-10pm.

El Pacifico, Calle San Nicolás e/ Zanja y Dragones, Central Havana, ph 63 3243 - open Tue-Sun noon-7pm - extremely popular with tourists and Cubans.

La Torre de Marfil, Calle Mercaderes e/ Obispo y Obrapía, Old Havana, ph 62 3466 - open every day noon-10pm - fun setting, good and friendly service.

Pavo Real, 7ma Ave No 205 e/ 2 y 4, Miramar, ph 33 2315 - open every day noon-midnight - delicious and inexpensive food.

Arabian

Almedina, Calle Oficios e/ Obrapía y Obispo, Old Havana, ph 63 0862 - open Thu-Tue noon-9pm.

Oasis, Prado No 258, Old Havana, ph 61 0582 - cheap and tasty, good lamb dishes and hummus, budget-travellers haunt.

Seafood

El Caribeño, cnr calles 21 and N, Vedado, ph 32 0383 - open Wed-Mon noon-10pm.

El Floridita, Calle Monserrate No 557, Old Havana, ph 63 1060 - open every day noon-1am - from 1930 to 1960, Hemingway occupied the corner barstool drinking copious cocktails and abusing unsuspecting patrons (which earned him the brickbat *'un saco de madarrias'* - a sack of shit), backdrop for his novel *An Island In The Stream*, the 'cradle of the *daiquiri'*, host to Gary Cooper, Tennessee Williams, Jean Paul Sartre, the Duke and Duchess of Windsor, recently refurbished, expensive food in restaurant at back, good cocktails, lots of camera-toting tourists.

La Terraza de Cojímar, Calle Real 161, Cojímar, ph 65 3471 - open every day noon-11pm.

La Zaragozana, Calle Monserrate e/ Obispo y Obrapía, Old Havana, ph 63 1062 - open every day noon-midnight - better and less expensive food than the nearby El Floridita.

Papas, Marina Hemingway, Calle 248 y 5ta Ave, Playa, ph 33 1150 - open every day noon-midnight - good shellfish, more Hemingway.

Snacks and Fast Food

Al Cappucino, cnr calles Oficios and Obispo, Old Havana - open every day - al fresco, good coffee, sandwiches, fries.

Café Paris, Calle Obispo No 202, Old Havana, ph 62 0466 - open every day 24 hours - fried chicken, toasted sandwiches, fries, live Cuban music.

Cafeteria Cubanitas, 5ta Ave e/ 40 y 42, Miramar, ph 33 2450 - open every day 7.30am-8.30pm - pizza.

Doña Isabel, cnr calles Tacón and Empedrado, Old Havana, ph 63 3560 - open every day 24 hours - baked chicken, spaghetti, sandwiches.

Dos Gardenias, Calle 7ma y 28, Miramar, ph 33 4186 - open every day noon-midnight - pizza.

La Fuente del Patio, Plaza de la Catedral, Old Havana, ph 61 8511 - open every day 24 hours - ice-cream, sandwiches.

La Lluvia de Oro, cnr calles Obispo and Habana, Old Havana - open every day 24 hours - steak sandwiches, spaghetti, pizza, coffee that tastes like diarrhoea, giant video screen showing latest pop and world music releases.

La Mina, Calle Obispo e/ Oficios y Mercaderes, Old Havana, ph 62 0216 - open every day 24 hours - al fresco, sandwiches, fries, live Cuban music (*Guantanamera* seems a particular favourite), good cocktails, service slow and uneven.

Los Marinos, Ave del Puerto y Obispo, Old Havana, ph 33 8808 - open every day 3pm-1am - sandwiches, fries.

Ice-cream

Coppelia, cnr calles 23 and L, Vedado - open every day 8am-10pm - sublime ice-cream, one of the best parlours in the world, inspired setting for much of the film *Strawberry and Chocolate*, Cubans line up for ages to buy a tub.

Coppelita, Calle 25 y Malecón, Vedado - open every day - Coppelia imitator but still good value.

El Narajal Cremeria, corner calles Cuba and Obispo, Old Havana - open every day - takeaway tubs, cakes and desserts.

There is another popular peso-only ice-cream parlour at Calle Obispo No 467 which is open every day.

Supermarkets

Some hotels, such as the Sevilla, have small supermarkets that stock biscuits, crackers, chocolate, alcohol, mineral water and fruit juice. The larger supermarkets - with every imaginable item - are in Miramar and include:

Diplomercado, Calle 3 y 7, ph 33 2198 - bring passport for identification.

Supermercado 70, corner Ave 3ra and Calle 70, ph 33 2890 - open Mon-Sat 9am-7pm Sun 9.30am-noon.

Supermercado Flores, Calle 176 e/ 1ra y 3ra, ph 33 6512 - open Mon-Fri 10am-6pm Sat-Sun 10am-2pm.

Market

There is a good market and food stall with fresh fruit and vegetables in Havana's Chinatown, cnr calles Zanja and Rajo, Central Havana. Payment is in pesos but bring dollars just in case.

Bakery

Panaderia San José, Calle Obispo, Old Havana - open every day - cheap pastries, rolls and bread sticks. Another good bakery is next to the Diplomercado in Miramar.

Entertainment

Cinemas

There are over 80 cinemas in Havana. Most usually show a sorry mix of dated Hollywood and Latin American fare but for first-run movies try:

Acapulco, Calle 26 e/ 35 y 37, Vedado.

Cine Charles Chaplin, Calle 23 e/ 10 y 12, Vedado.

Cine 23 y 12, Calle 12 y 23, Vedado.

La Rampa, Calle 23 e/ O y P, Vedado.

Payret, Prado No 503, Old Havana.

Yara, Calle 23 y L, Vedado.

Theatres

Performances throughout the week generally begin around 8.30pm while Sunday shows are held at 5pm and 8pm. Havana's best theatres are:

El Sótano, Calle K e/ 25 y 27, Vedado, ph 32 0630 - good range of modern Cuban plays.

Gran Teatro de la Habana, Prado y San Rafael, Central Havana, ph 61 3078 - excellent setting in the city's best theatre, ballet, opera and theatre, home of the National Ballet of Cuba.

Hubert de Blanck, Calle Calzada e/ A y B, Vedado, ph 30 1011 - classical and more contemporary plays.

Karl Marx, Ave 1ra e/ 8 y 10, Miramar, ph 30 0720 - national and international performances.

HAVANA

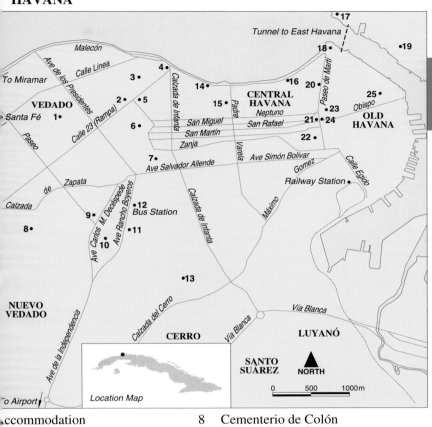

Accommodation
- Capri
- Nacional de Cuba
- Habana Libre
- 6 Deauville
- 0 Caribbean
- 1 Inglaterra
- 3 Plaza

Other
- Museo de Artes Decorativos
- Coppelia
- University of Havana
- Parque Quinta de los Molinos

8   Cementerio de Colón
9   Teatro Nacional
10   Plaza de la Revolución
11   Biblioteca Nacional
12   Bus Station
13   Latin-American Stadium
14   Parque Maceo
15   Hermanos Ameijeiras Hospital
17   Castillo del Morro
18   Castillo de San Salvador de la Punta
19   Castillo de San Carlos de la Cabaña
22   Capitolio Nacional
24   Parque Central
25   Plaza de la Catedral

OLD HAVANA

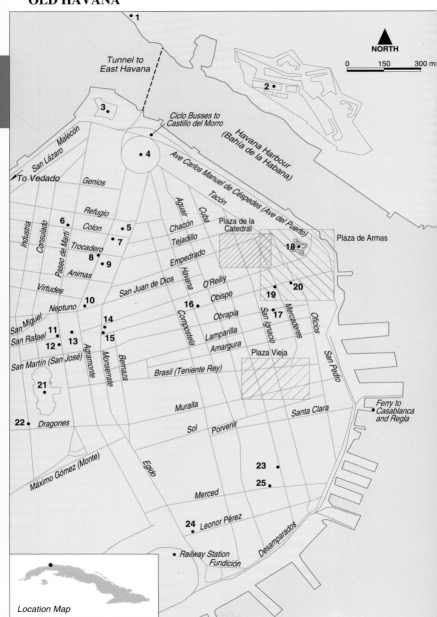

NORTH

0   150   300 m

Tunnel to
East Havana

Ciclo Busses to
Castillo del Morro

Havana Harbour
(Bahía de la Habana)

Malecón

San Lázaro

To Vedado

Genios

Refugio

Ave Carlos Manuel de Céspedes (Ave del Puerto)

Tacón

Aguiar

Cuba

Chacón

Plaza de la
Catedral

Plaza de Armas

Colon

Industria

Consulado

Paseo de Martí

Trocadero

Tejadillo

Empedrado

Animas

Havana

San Juan de Dios

O'Reilly

Obispo

Obrapía

Lamparilla

Amargura

San Ignacio

Mercaderes

Oficios

Virtudes

Neptuno

San Miguel

San Rafael

Compostela

San Martín (San José)

Agramonte

Monserrate

Bernaza

Brasil (Teniente Rey)

Plaza Vieja

San Pedro

Ferry to
Casablanca
and Regla

Dragones

Muralla

Sol

Porvenir

Santa Clara

Máximo Gómez (Monte)

Egido

Merced

Leonor Pérez

Railway Station
Fundición

Desamparados

Location Map

Mella, Calle Línea y A, Vedado, ph 38696 - modern and traditional folk dancing, plays, variety galas.

Teatro Nacional, Calle Línea y A, Vedado, ph 79 6011 - symphonic music, opera, plays and variety shows.

Nightclubs and Cabarets

All the main hotels, such as the Nacional de Cuba, Habana Libre, Riviera, Capri and Inglaterra, have their own nightclubs but admission and drinks aren't cheap ($10 admission; $7 for drinks). The music is a combination of Western techno and Cuban *salsa* and the crowds a mix of backpackers and Spanish tourists - all tans and burliness - to *jiniteras* in skimpy bodice-rippers.

The Tropicana, Calle 72 No 4504, Marianao, ph 20 5114, is Havana's most famous nightclub. It is also the biggest with seating and standing for over 1000 patrons. The shows, reminiscent of the colourful extravaganzas of Las Vegas, feature more than 200 scantily-clad chorus girls - stilettoed and wearing enormous headdresses - who take to the stage, accompanied by singers, musicians and an orchestra. The highlight of the evening is a routine called the 'Dancing Chandeliers', where a line of dancers appear sporting brightly-lit lamps on their heads. Its quite something, believe me.

The Tropicana offers two shows a night: the main performance runs for almost two hours and ends around 11pm; a second begins at midnight and finishes at 1am. There's also a snack shop, a rather dull souvenir store and packs of *jiniteras* saying 'Have you heard from your brother in Miami?'. Bookings are essential and can be made through

KEY TO MAP

- ACCOMMODATION
- 6 Caribbean
- 8 Sevilla
- 10 Plaza
- 11 Inglaterra
- 19 Ambos Mundos

- EATING
- 14 El Floritida
- 15 La Zaragozana
- 16 La Lluvia de Oro
- 20 La Mina

- OTHER
- 1 Castillo del Morro
- 2 Castillo de San Carlos de la Cabana
- 3 Castillo de San Salvador de la Punta
- 4 Statue of Máximo Gómez
- 5 Museo de la Revolución
- 7 Granma Memorial
- 9 Museo Nacional de Bellas Artes
- 12 Gran Teatro de la Habana
- 13 Parque Central
- 17 Casa de Africa
- 18 El Castillo de la Real Fuerza
- 21 Capitolio Nacional
- 22 Partagás Cigar Factory
- 23 Iglesia Parroquial del Espiritu Santo
- 24 Casa Natal de José Martí
- 25 Iglesia y Convento de la Merced

Cubatur or major hotels. Entry is expensive, ranging from $30 for a show, glass of wine and cheap seats to $78 for a show, glass of wine, bottle of rum and front-row seats.

For something a little less glitzy, try the *Arcos de Cristal*, next door to the Tropicana, which has live and taped music to 2am, and the *El Galeón*, a floating disco/restaurant with two dance floors that leaves from the dock near the Castillo del Morro (tickets are $10 and can be purchased from the boat or the Havana Libre Hotel).

Bars

Local bars such as *El Bibao*, cnr calles O'Reilly and Aguiar, Old Havana, provide some of the best entertainment in Havana. The music is loud and Caribbean-tinged, the hours flexible, the drinks cheap and the customers a vigorous jumble of taxi drivers, musicians and *bomberos* (firemen). Payment is usually in dollars even though Cubans pay in pesos.

Most hotels and restaurants have bars. Outside of these try:

Bar Castillo de la Real Fuerza, Calle O'Reilly y Tacón, Old Havana, ph 61 6130.

Club 21, cnr calles 21 and N, Vedado, ph 32 9602.

Club Los Marinos, Ave del Puerto y Obispo, Old Havana, ph 33 8808.

Piano Bar el Patio, cnr calles San Ignacio and Empedrado, Old Havana, ph 61 8504.

Río Club, cnr calles 3ra and O, Miramar, ph 29 3399.

Music and Dance

Good Cuban jazz can be heard at the popular *Maxim Club*, Calle 10, Vedado, ph 33981. The *Riviera Hotel*, *Café Paris* and *La Mina* also feature live jazz. Performances of Afro-Cuban music and dance by the *National Folklore Group* can be seen at Calle 4 e/ Calzaday y 5, Vedado.

Shopping

Havana's main shopping streets include calles Galiano, San Rafael, Neptuno and Calzada de Infanta - all in Central Havana - where you can buy clothing, shoes, cheap souvenirs and curios. Calle Obispo, Old Havana and Calle 23, Vedado have Cuban art, handicrafts, clothing, posters, books, music cassettes and CDs plus the largest stocks of Ché paraphernalia in Havana.

Foodstuffs, juices, tobacco, alcohol, clothing, jewellery, musical instruments, shoes, postcards, stamps, film, maps and electrical goods can be found in most major hotels, Caracol and Infotur branches, as well as dollar stores.

Cigars and Rum

Casa del Tabaco, corner calles Quinta and 16, Miramar - excellent range of cigars.

Casa del Ron, Calle Monserrate No 557, Old Havana (above the El Floritida restaurant) - rum and plenty of it.

Partagás, Calle Industria (behind the Capitolo), Old Havana - a shop inside the factory sells Cuban cigars and rum at good prices, Cohibas (boxes of 25) from $39-414, friendly and very informative service, infrequent tours to see the cigar-making process.

Books, Music, Art and Souvenirs

Artex, Calle L y 23, Vedado - books including some English-language titles, handicrafts, jewellery, CDs, cassettes, posters and postcards.

Bazar-Aborigenes, Calle Berarza e/ Obispo y O'Reilly, Old Havana - good selection of tapestries, books, posters and wood carvings.

Bazar Plaza Vieja, Calle San Ignacio e/ Rey y Muralla, Old Havana - reproductions and souvenirs.

Casa de la Miniatura, cnr calles Tacón and Empedrado, Old Havana - pricey miniature chess pieces and boards, T-shirts, good straw hats.

Egrem's House of Music, cnr calles 20 No 3308 and 35, Miramar - the best selection of Cuban music and musical instruments in Havana.

Fondo Cuban de Bienes Culturales, Calle Muralla y San Ignacio, Old Havana - textiles, ceramics, gold and silver work, leather goods.

Forma, Calle Obispo No 255, Old Havana - excellent but expensive Cuban and expressionist sculpture.

Galería del Grabado, Plaza de la Catedral, Old Havana - lithographs, graphics and paintings by local artists.

La Exposición, Centro Commercial Mazana de Gómez, Old Havana - huge selection of graphics, posters, Afro-Cuban art - ask to look at their range downstairs.

La Internacional, Calle Obispo No 528, Old Havana - English-language titles, magazines, posters and postcards.

Palacio de Artesanía, Calle Cuba No 64, Old Havana - three-floors of shops selling expensive clothing (the rare and highly prized Hatuey beer T-shirts are a good buy but check availability), cigars, alcohol, handicrafts, Cuban music and musical instruments, books and maps.

Palacio del Arte, cnr calles 72 and 5ta Ave, Miramar - works of art, furniture.

Taller de Pintura, Calle Obispo No 312, Old Havana - paintings, graphics and objet dart.

WSP, Calle 33 No 2003 e/ 20 y 22, Playa - Cuban and international music cassettes and CDs.

Poster Art

Cuban political, educational and filmic posters are stuck up everywhere on the city's walls or on specially designated poster stands. Designs are catholic in taste - from Pop Art to Constructivism to Surrealism - and are generally executed as silkscreens.

Originals are sometimes auctioned in Old Havana (watch out for the signs advertising the location of their sale), while good quality reproductions are sold ($10-15) in the city's tourist stores and art galleries.

Clothing

La Maison, cnr calles 16 N 701 and 7ma Ave, Miramar - the place where Havana's sartorial come to shop. Inside is an impressive array of expensive clothes for men and women plus cigars, alcohol, jewellery, perfume, leather goods, and arts and crafts. Evenings are usually reserved for fashion shows trumpeting exclusive designer and ready-to-wear collections.

Popa PaRampa, cnr calles 23 and P, Vedado - colourful Cuban fashions.

Sightseeing

Havana is crammed with museums. Museums for everything - Afro-Cuban art and artefacts, European painting and sculpture, national and international writers, history, past and present. While admission to many of them, and other attractions, is relatively cheap ($1-5), taking photographs or video recording events can balloon costs (expect to pay an extra $5 for photographs and up to $30 for recordings). There is also no student discount to any of the sights.

Old Havana (Habana Vieja)

Within the boundaries of the old colonial core, in the north-eastern pocket of Havana, stand some of the finest buildings and monuments built in Cuba between the 16th and 19th centuries. Because of this historical wealth, UNESCO designated Old Havana a World Heritage Site in 1982, lavishing millions of dollars on its restoration.

Often touted as a 'living museum', Old Havana seems more like a bomb site these days with its scaffolded buildings and streets filled with hurriedly junked piles of sand and cement. Although the government has restored over 90 of the most important buildings, renovations are slow and hindered by lack of resources (UNESCO money has since dried up). Among this muddle of work are rows of dishevelled apartments where over 100,000 people continue to live.

Houses of Cards

Nearly 50% of Havana's buildings have been described as being in a mediocre or poor condition, with a significant number beyond repair. Unfortunately, the historical site of Old Havana has suffered the worse deterioration. According to one resident, 'living in the area is to live with a constant fear that on a rainy day you will return home and find only ruins'.

Yet despite the obvious destruction, Old Havana is without doubt the most interesting part of the city. Even the shortest of tours will reveal glimpses of former brilliance: delightful squares; colonial mansions and palaces; gracious architecture. The quarter is well laid-out in a grid pattern and rarely confusing, and most attractions can be easily seen in a day.

The Plaza de la Catedral, in the north-eastern section of Old Havana, is considered the city's most beautiful square (a fact not lost on the makers of Havana's first music video - *Silk Pyjamas* by English singer Thomas Dolby). It is also an ideal place to begin a walking tour. On weekends, the square is hostage to crowded exhibitions of Cuban handicrafts, street-sweepers who turn their task into a ceremony, and slow-moving groups of tourists.

La Catedral, with its tasteful, late-Baroque facade, was originally constructed in 1748, and dominates the northern end of the square. Inside are paintings and sculptures with a lavishly decorated main altar attracting most onlookers' attention. The alleged remains of Christopher Columbus were kept here for veneration until the end of Spanish rule, when they were shipped back to Spain. The cathedral still holds services and is best visited in the morning before midday.

At the southern end of the square is **El Palacio de los Condes de Casa-Bayona** (1720), one of the oldest buildings in the city, and the site of the **Museo de Arte Colonial**. The museum has showrooms filled with furniture, ornaments, metalwork, and one of Cuba's best collections of stained glass. The **Palacio del Conde Lombillio** (1737), on the square's eastern side, houses a teachers' museum while alongside is **El Palacio de los Marqueses de Arcos** (1741), a former gathering place for Havana's wealthy and now the location of a graphic arts school.

To the west of the square is the **Antigua Casa de Baños**. This building originally housed a water tank (the city's residents and Spanish ships would draw from its source); today it is an art gallery and handicrafts store. Nearby is **La Casa del Conde de la Reunion,** which has an interesting cultural centre, and a lovely patio surrounded by balconies festooned with colourful fabric.

Plaza de Armas, a short stroll south-east of the **Plaza de la Catedral,** is the city's oldest square although it wasn't fully completed until the late 18th century. Formerly the headquarters of Havana's highest-ranking political and military leaders, it's now a centre of a more egalitarian kind. The square's park, cooled by overhanging trees and palms, is an inviting place to seek respite from the sun, eat ice-cream, chat to the locals and ward off spruikers handing out flyers from the local restaurants. Trysting lovers are a common sight at night, when big iron lamp posts provide the park's lighting.

El Castillo de la Real Fuerza (1558-77), north of the square, is the oldest fort in Havana and reputedly the second oldest fort built by the Spanish in the New World. Once the residence of the island's colonial governors, then a military garrison, it now houses a number of art exhibitions. The bell tower of the fort is topped by an elegant weathervane (a replica; the original blew off in a hurricane) of a woman holding the cross of Calatrava. Known as **'La Giraldilla',** it is the city's unofficial symbol. Cast in 1631, the weathervane is a tribute to the wife of Cuban Governor Hernando de Soto, who had set off to explore the south-eastern coast of the USA. She waited patiently for De Soto's return but her vigil proved in vain - soon after discovering the Mississippi River, he was supposedly struck down and eaten by cannibals. Entrance to the fort, which has recently been refurbished, is via a debris-cluttered moat.

North-east of the square is the neoclassical **El Templete** (construction began in 1827). Built in honour of the city's founding, it is also the place where Havana's first settlers celebrated Mass (a ceiba tree marks the spot). Inside are paintings by the French painter Jean Baptiste Vermay (a pupil of the 18th century neoclassical painter Jacques-Louis David) and a vase containing the remains of the artist and his wife. Nearby is the 19th-century **Palacio del Conde Santovenia.** Designed for a Count, the palace gained widespread infamy for holding the bawdiest parties in Havana. At the time of writing, it was closed for renovation.

Walking west, the colonnaded **Palacio de los Capitanes Generales** (1776-91) is one of the most beautiful and important architectural monuments in the city. Completed in 1791, the building was used as the residence of the captain general as well as the island's colonial governors. After that it became the seat of the Cuban government, and from 1920 the headquarters of the local municipal authorities. In 1967 it underwent extensive refurbishment and is today the location of the **Museo de la Ciudad** (admission is $3; tickets are also available to see all of Old Havana's museums for $9) containing a variety of statues, paintings, furniture, memorabilia from the wars of independence and the original La Giraldilla weathervane. The interior patio, thronged with ornamental plants and shrubbery, holds a white statue of Christopher Columbus made in 1826; on one side is the '*El Fuerte*' cannon, once an integral part of the city's defences. Most days the outside arcade is filled with booksellers and their stalls - the novels of Gabriel García Márquez preponderate (in Spanish only).

Immediately north is the **Palacio del Segundo Cabo**, a building of more sombre design, that has served as a post office, law courts and an academy. It is now home to a reasonably good bookshop.

Calle Obispo, immediately south of the square, is one of Havana's most elegant streets: cobble road surfaces; latticed screens on the shop windows; carved wooden doors large enough to drive a car through. It was once known as 'the street of bookshops' until most were closed by Castro's government (one of the survivors, the excellent La Moderna Poesia, has unfortunately also moved away). Calle Obispo is also where the restoration of Old Havana first began. Today it's a blend of al fresco cafés (all located in the eastern part of Calle Obispo that has recovered its former colonial glory), souvenir stores, craft workshops, bakeries, ice-cream parlours and wondrous old pharmacies, their shelves lined with enormous medicinal jars. Perfect for serendipitous exploring, the street is an obligatory excursion for every visitor to Havana. On the corner of calles Obispo and Mercaderes is the famous **Ambos Mundos Hotel.** Ernest Hemingway once lived here, in a scruffy room on the fifth floor. It was here that he wrote *To Have and Have Not*, his first Cuban novel, and where he started *For Whom the Bell Tolls*. He would set out from the hotel, dressed in slacks and *guayabera*, for the *La Floridita* restaurant where he drank daiquiris when he was at a loose end. Apparently Hemingway so loved Havana that he wanted to stay forever. But the Revolution put paid to his wishes and he was forced to move away. When he left, his room was preserved (and tidied, one can only assume) with his typewriter and a few personal knick-knacks kept out on display. At the time of writing, the building was closed for extensive renovations and is not due to reopen until early 1996.

A block south, on Calle Obrapía, is the **Casa de Africa**, one of the best museums in Havana to see Afro-Cuban artefacts.

Four blocks south of Calle Obispo, along Calle Mercaderes, is the **Plaza Vieja** (Old Square). During the 17th and 18th centuries, the square was Havana's main centre of commerce but today it is hard to see why (admittedly, the building of an underground parking lot hasn't helped matters). Plaza Vieja does, however, have a few architectural treasures; excellent acoustics also makes it a popular spot for outdoor concerts. Just off the square are two impressive buildings: the **Casa de Esteban José Portier** and the **Casa de Franchi Alfaro**, both beautifully restored.

South of the square is the **Casa de los Condes de Jaruco** (1733-77), which displays all the features synonymous with an exclusive Havana residence: patio filled with royal palms, spacious parlours, and lots of polished wood. The building was restored in 1979 and is now the **Fondo Cubano de Bienes Culturales**, a popular setting for art and cultural exhibitions. The enormous **Convento de Santa Clara** (1638-44), further south, was the first convent built in Cuba, then an abattoir, and today houses the offices of those involved in Old Havana's restoration. Another block south is the **Iglesia Parroquial del Espíritu Santo** (1632), the oldest church in Havana. Services are held each Sunday. And two blocks south of here, on the corner of calles Cuba and Merced, is the **Iglesia y Convento de la Merced**, where white-robed *Santería* worshippers are a common sight at prayer.

Walking south, then turning left on Calle Leonor Pérez for six blocks, is the **Casa Natal de José Martí**. This innocuous, two-storey house holds a pivotal place in Cuban history - it is the birthplace, on 28 January 1853, of Cuba's favourite son, José Martí. During the 1960s the house was completely revamped; neighbouring buildings were also demolished and a more fitting park built in their place. Inside is a hagiography of his life, and a collection of his personal effects. Immediately west is the gigantic and chaotic **Central Railway Station**. The highlight here is watching vintage American cars (Buicks, Chevys, Fords, Hudsons, Packards and Studebakers) chug up, unload and pick-up passengers.

Walking north, along Calle Egido then turning left on Calle Máximo Gómez, brings you to **Paseo del Martí** (more commonly known as the Prado). Built in 1772 and similar in design to its famous namesake in Madrid, the Prado is a graceful old street with a broad central esplanade: laurel-lined with marble benches. Most days, the benches are occupied by men trading goods or gabbing about what a bankrupt, brainwashed country Cuba has become. School children, dressed in crisp uniforms of maroon shorts and white shirts, shout at passing tourists ('Hey mister! Where you from! You give me money!') and romp about whooping and waving. Later in the afternoon, the esplanade is under siege as the children, freed from lessons, whoosh along on makeshift carts.

Flanking the Prado are lovingly restored hotels and scurf-infested apartments, theatres, souvenir stalls, and refreshment stops. Being sooled by touts and *jineteras* is a common problem here.

At the south end of the Prado stands the luminescent **Capitolio Nacional** (1926-9). If the building looks familiar, that's because its modelled on Washington's Capitol and the Congress Building in Buenos Aires. Over 2000 workers were involved in its immoderate construction (at a cost of $17 million) which takes up almost an entire block. Dominating the interior - beneath the centre of a ceilinged dome - is an enormous bronze statue of an armed woman which represents the Republic of Cuba. It is also considered one of the largest indoor sculptures in the world. Formerly the seat of the House of Representatives, it is now home to the **Academy of Sciences** and a museum devoted to the island's flora and fauna. Entrance is to the left of the main staircase.

Further north is the splendid **Gran Teatro de la Habana** (1915), the city's leading theatre. Heavily adorned by columns, sculptures and entablature, the theatre is reputed to be one of the largest in the world with a seating capacity for over 2000. Some of this century's greatest talents have performed here including the actress Sarah Bernhardt and the tenor Enrico Caruso. Cuba's celebrated National Opera and National Ballet now hold performances in the theatre. Across the street is the **Parque Central**, which displays a statue of José Martí (1905), who looks like he's about to deliver the Sermon on the Mount, in the centre.

Walking north along Calle Monseratte for a few hundred metres brings you to the **Museo Nacional de Bellas Artes**. One of the country's best cultural museums, it boasts collections of Cuban and European paintings (purportedly by Velázquez, Van Dyck and Tintoretto among others) as well as art and artefacts from more ancient times. Opposite, on the other side of Calle Colón, is the Presidential Palace, now the **Museo de la Revolución**. Inside are spacious but gloomy old rooms with exhibits of a strongly nationalistic bent. (Decoration is by Tiffanys of New York though you wouldn't know it standing among the collected detritus of battle.) A display on the second floor shows wax dummies of Fidel and the rebels in poses of hirsute aggravation; each are spotlessly dressed but their enemies, including the Americans, are less so. Some - I had to look twice - appeared to be sweating. On the ground floor is 'Cretins Corner', featuring effigies of Fulgencio Batista and Ronald Reagan. ('Thank you, cretin', says the sign to Batista, 'for helping us to make the Revolution', and another telling Reagan, 'Thank you, cretin, for helping strengthen the Revolution'.) Also on the same floor, just down the corridor, are tired, revolutioned-out staff selling cheap coffee and souvenirs.

Included in the admission price ($3; no cameras are allowed inside) is entrance to the *Granma Memorial*, the yacht that bore Castro and his men from Mexico in 1956 to the island's south-eastern coast. Protected by glass casing (bullet-proofing?), the *Granma* is surrounded by various objects such as bits of planes, jeeps, and weapons used in the revolutionary fight. The white-walled **Iglesia Santo Angel Custodia** (1695), where José Martí was baptised, is nearby. The building, recently restored, is one of the most beautiful churches in Havana.

Further north, along Calle Zulueta, is the **Parque de los Mártires**. It's a small, drab park with a monument dedicated to eight medical students who were executed for trashing the grave of a Spanish writer. Facing east is a bronze statue of Máximo Gómez, the Dominican-born general who was one of the leaders of Cuba's independence from Spain. And near the statue are the barely discernible remains of the old **city prison** (1834-8), which once held a number of Cuban revolutionaries, including José Martí.

The **Castillo de San Salvador de la Punta** (1589) stands at the end of the Prado. Designed by the Italian engineer Juan Bautista Antonelli, it was one in a series of forts built to add oomph to the city's defences. Afternoon concerts (with blaring disco music) are usually held here, much to the chagrin of the local fishermen.

Central Havana (Centro)

West of Old Havana, across the Prado, is the neighbourhood of Central Havana. Before the Revolution it was the city's red-light district but today its more a pale pastel - an area of badly rutted streets, near-feral dogs and clapped-out cars rusting away at kerbside. Street life is dominated by men slumped in doorways smoking cigars and laughing *hijos* (children) playing basketball or kicking around flattened footballs. Often avoided by travellers, Central Havana has a few worthwhile sights including a busy and colourful thoroughfare, and one of Havana's most popular weekend destinations.

The **Malecón**, the seawall skirting Central Havana's northern boundary, is where many *habaneros* (Havana residents) come to swim, sunbathe, scull rum or leisurely stroll arm-in-arm. Bicycles, some preposterously overloaded (I saw four adults and children on one bicycle, and a passenger on another carrying an enormous black and white television set) dash in and out of traffic; men wrestle with inner tubes before setting out for a day's fishing on the bay; and across the street, multiple tenancies - suffering years of neglect and battered by tropical storms that periodically rake the coast - are falling down faster than the authorities can repair them.

For mine, a walk along the Malecón is easily the most fascinating and enjoyable way to while away an afternoon.

West along the Malecón is the **Parque Maceo**, which is dominated by an impressive statue of Antonio Maceo, the moustachioed general who fought alongside Máximo Gómez and José Martí in the wars of independence. The skyscraper behind the park is the **Hermanos Ameijeiras Hospital**, one of the best medical institutions in Cuba, and the place where overseas patients come for their organ transplants.

Central Havana's busiest shopping precinct is **Calle San Rafael** which begins from the Prado then extends several blocks into the heart of the neighbourhood. This is a popular Cuban beat of 'dollar stores' (the queues are a dead giveaway), open-air barbers (payment in pesos), peanut-sellers, shonky old cinemas, and ad hoc markets selling everything from snacks and metal belts to car parts and cooking utensils. Also in the vicinity is Havana's **Chinatown**. Now somewhat run-down, it possesses a number of cheap foodstalls, and has an excellent fruit and vegetable market.

Vedado

Havana's bustling residential district, Vedado lies further west of Central Havana and extends all the way to the Río Almendares. Modelled on Miami, the area once reeked of money and narcotics: during the late 1950s, it was the playground of mobsters, movie stars, penny-ante poker players and prostitutes. Things are considerably less colourful today, but Vedado still boasts some of the city's best hotels and nightspots as well as a fair modicum of sights.

On the corner of calles San Miguel and Ronda is the **Museo Napoleónico**. While the connection between the little French general and Cuba is tenuous (apparently his personal physician was Cuban), the museum has a slavish collection of books, photographs and personal belongings pertaining to Napoleonic lore. A block west is the **University of Havana**, an impressive group of neoclassical buildings dominated by a wide, sweeping staircase. Among its graduates are Carlos Manuel de Céspedes, Ignacio Agramonte and Fidel Castro (who failed to be elected president of the students' federation). The campus was originally established in Old Havana during the early

18th century, and moved to its present site in 1902.

South of the university is the **Plaza de la Revolución**. This sprawling, eerily empty square (it's only ever full during national celebrations) houses the governments ministries, and has as its focus, the enormous **Monumento á José Martí**. Further south is the charmless **Palacio de la Revolución**, enlivened only by a mural of Ché Guevara, where Castro reputedly holes up during his working day. The guards here are incredibly paranoid - when I pulled out a map to get my bearings, two ran over and brusquely asked me to leave (perhaps they mistook me for a spy). Flanking the square is the **Teatro Nacional**, a venue for classical music and plays, and the **Biblioteca Nacional**, which houses the country's largest collection of books and manuscripts.

Returning north, then turning right on Ave Salvador Allende, brings you to the **Parque Quinta de los Molinos**. Overgrown and in need of repair, the park is still a lovely place to sit in the shade and relax. Jazz musicians and dance groups from the local conservatory come to practise here and no one (I kid you not) will stop you for soap.

Vedado's two other sights are a little more spread out so a car or taxi may be required to move between them. On Calle 17, between calles D and E, is the sumptuous **Museo de Artes Decorativos** which houses an exquisite collection of ornamental wall hangings, china and antique furniture. And near the corner of calles 23 and 12 is Havana's pre-eminent burial site - the **Cementerio de Colón**. Beyond the main entrance is an outstanding display of funerary architecture including luxurious mausoleums, sculptures, and a magnificent colonnade topped by a set of writing tablets.

Miramar

Stretching west from the Río Almendares, Miramar was once the exclusive district of Havana. It remains an up-scale neighbourhood of wide avenues occupied by foreign embassies, expensive stores, lavishly restored mansions and the odd, abandoned villa thrown in for revolutionary balance. Streams of late-model cars cruise **Quinta Avenida**, the main drag, while Miami Vice look-alikes cluster on the pavement. Miramar is not endowed with many sights; instead most travellers come here to shop.

For spy buffs and anyone with a hankering for James Bond movies, the **Museo del Ministerio de Interior**, is well worth a few hours of your time. Whether intentional or not, the exhibits are a delightful mixture of badinage and black humour - gadgets, weapons and farcical plots to assassinate Castro. The museum, housed in a modest building, is on the corner of Quinta and Calle 14.

At the end of Quinta Avenida is the **Acuario Nacional**. Founded in 1960, the aquarium has recently been enlarged but it's still a little tatty - feeding time at the Moray eel enclosure is fun to watch though.

The **Marina Hemingway** is further west, along Quinta Avenida and past the Río Jaimanitas. An amorphous tourist resort, it's filled with hotels, restaurants, shops, tennis courts and moorings for over 600 yachts. Each year the marina hosts the Ernest Hemingway Marlin Classic fishing tournament, which attracts lots of visitors from the USA.

Outlying Attractions

South of Havana is a vast recreational space known as **Parque Lenin** (6 sq km). Completed in 1970, it contains an amphitheatre, craft workshop, race track, rodeo, amusement rides (which weren't operating at the time of writing), pool plus a few foodstalls. To avoid the crowds, the park is best visited during the week. About a kilometre west is the **National Zoo**. The animals aren't caged but most look the worse for wear. Some of the animals actually looked dead. A much better excursion is to the **National Botanical Gardens** (6 sq km), south of the zoo, which holds over 100,000 plant species including orchids and cacti. Attractively laid out, the enclosure also comprises ponds and small waterfalls, bridges and decorated buildings. Nearby is **Expocuba**, an enormous centre that highlights the country's achievements in science, agriculture, the arts, etc.

East of Havana lay impressive forts, reasonable beaches, inexpensive resorts, and immortalised fishing villages. A tunnel - almost one kilometre long - crosses under the entrance to Havana Harbour to the daunting **Castillo del Morro** (1589-1630). Designed by Antonelli (the same man who drew up the plans for the Castillo de San Salvador de la Punta across the bay), the fort was originally considered unconquerable, until it was attacked and stormed by the English in 1762. It has since been used as a prison, and now houses a maritime museum, souvenir stores and cafés. The views over the Malecón and Old Havana from the ramparts are spectacular. Needless to say, the fort has been damned to endless appearances in tourist brochures and on postcards.

Adjacent to here is another craggy bulwark, the **Castillo de San Carlos de la Cabaña** (1763-74). It's nowhere near as impressive as the **Castillo del Morro**, although it does have a good museum, with most attention focused on Cuba's exporting of revolutionary socialism to Africa. The loud noise you hear every evening (9pm on the dot) is a cannon being fired from its grounds.

East of these two forts is the **Pan-American Village and Stadium**, built for the 1991 Pan-American Games by a volunteer labour force including members of the national athletics team. (Cuba topped the medal count that year so the extra work obviously didn't do the athletes any harm.) Nearby is the weather-beaten fishing village of **Cojímar** which featured in Hemingway's acclaimed novel *The Old Man and the Sea*. Travellers and tour groups usually make a beeline to the *La Terraza de Cojímar* restaurant overlooking the harbour. The seafood is excellent and there's plenty of reminders of Hemingway to keep the conversation flowing. Forget about swimming here; the coastline is rocky and fouled by pollution. A taxi from Havana to Cojímar will cost around $10.

After Cojímar is the district of Alamar, followed by Celimar, another fishing village. There is little to recommend in either of them. East of Celimar is **Playa del Este**, a budget resort covering 10km of beaches.

Beached

The volcanic shoreline of Cojímar has been the unlikely locale of a quite awesome spectacle - it was here, in 1994, that hundreds of *balseros* attempted to escape the island by sea. Their choice of craft was desperate: inner tubes, rafts, engine-powered skiffs, bathtubs, and in one instance, a boat made from a man's bed.

Bacuranao, the first of the beaches, *Santa María del Mar* and *Guanabo* all have excellent diving (eight dive sites have been marked along Playe del Este) while a range of watersports, including water skiing and wind surfing, are also available. Taxis from Havana to any of these beaches will cost up to $20.

Inland are the pleasant colonial towns of **Guanabacoa** and **Santa María del Rosario**. The principal sight at the former is the **Museo Histórico de Guanabacoa**, Calle Martí 108 between calles San Antonio and Versalles, which houses an excellent collection of Afro-Cuban religious art, while the latter has an interesting church that has a number of paintings, including one by Veronese.

The town of **San Francisco de Paula**, south of Gunabacoa, is where Hemingway lived with his wife, the American writer Martha Gellhorn, until the Revolution. They bought a simple, one-storey house here - the Finca Vigía - after falling in love with its views and palm-filled location. Now preserved as the **Museo Hemingway** (I wasn't permitted entry at the time of writing, but this policy may have changed), it contains rooms littered with stuffed animal heads, hunting weapons, books, papers, and the desk where he finished writing *For Whom the Bell Tolls*. If the museum is closed, you can peek through the windows or explore the lovely grounds (apparently the acres of long grass hide the owners' discarded bottles of gin). Hemingway's much-loved boat, *Pilar*, is berthed outside.

Further along the coast are **Jibacoa** and **Trópico**, both good snorkelling beaches. On the way you pass through the coastal village of Santa Cruz del Norte, where Ronera Santa Cruz, Cuba's largest rum factory and maker of Havana Club, is located.

Tours

In Cuba, tours are often the cheapest and easiest way of getting to/from a destination. All large hotels and tourist offices arrange tours, which can be half-day and one-day visits or excursions spanning several days. Meals, drinks and accommodation are provided for overnight stays and guides are knowledgeable and fluent in English, French and German.

Some of the more interesting tours in and around Havana include a tour of the city ($10), a drink and show at the *Tropicana* nightclub, night fishing and safaris, and visits to the beaches east of the city. *Partagás*, Cuba's longest-running cigar factory, has irregular and fascinating tours to see the cigar-making, packaging and labelling process. They usually start at 10am and cost $10 (the price includes a small pack of cigars and a drink).

Prices to destinations outside Havana include:

Varadero - $27.
Soroa - $29.
Vinales - $39.
Trinidad - $79.
Cayo Largo - $94.
Santiago de Cuba - $139.
Baracoa - $159.

Sports and Recreation

The Havana Golf Club, Calle de Vento km 8, Rpto, Capdevila R Boyero, has golf links, tennis courts plus a range of training facilities with instructors on call. **Tennis** can also be played at the *Nacional de Cuba* and *Neptuno-Tritóon* hotels; ask at reception for prices, availability and times.

If you need a workout, there's a good **gym** at the *Sala Polivalente Kid*

Chocolate, Prado e/ San José y Teniente Rey, Old Havana.

A number of hotels including *Sevilla*, *Comodoro* and the *Riviera* have **pools** open to foreigners; ask at reception for prices.

Baseball can be seen at the Latin-American Stadium, Calle Zequeira No 302 e/ Patria y Saravia, Cerro; **soccer** at the Pedro Marrero Stadium, Ave 41 No 4409 e/ 44 y 50, Cerro; and **rodeo shows** at the Parque Lenin, Calle Cortina de las Presa y Carretera del Globo. Other sporting events are held at the *Centro de Entrenamiento*, Prado No 207 e/ Refugio y Trocadero, Old Havana and *Cento Deportiva 'José Martí'*, corner calles G and Malecón, Vedado.

Basketball Players, Old Havana.

VARADERO

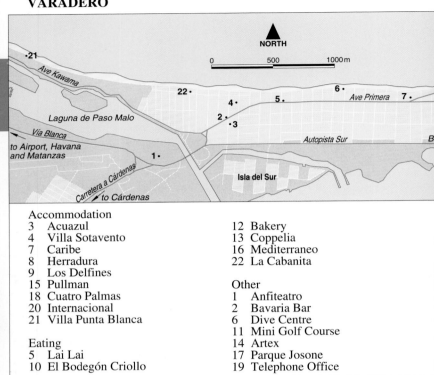

Accommodation
3 Acuazul
4 Villa Sotavento
7 Caribe
8 Herradura
9 Los Delfines
15 Pullman
18 Cuatro Palmas
20 Internacional
21 Villa Punta Blanca

Eating
5 Lai Lai
10 El Bodegón Criollo

12 Bakery
13 Coppelia
16 Mediterraneo
22 La Cabanita

Other
1 Anfiteatro
2 Bavaria Bar
6 Dive Centre
11 Mini Golf Course
14 Artex
17 Parque Josone
19 Telephone Office

EAST HAVANA BEACHES

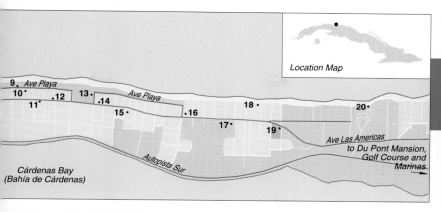

9. Ave Playa
10.
.12
13.
11.
.14
Ave Playa
15.
.16
18.
20.
17.
19.

Ave Las Americas
to Du Pont Mansion,
Golf Course and
Marinas

Cárdenas Bay
(Bahía de Cárdenas)

Autopista Sur

CUBA - PROVINCES

Pinar del Río

Havana

Matanzas

Villa Clara

Cienfuegos

Sancti Spíritus

Ciego de
Avila

Camagüey

Las Tunas

Holguín

Granma

Santiago
de Cuba

Guantánamo

Playa Boca Ciega

Playa Guanabo

Primera

Ave Tercera

Ave Quinta

Ave Quinta

BOCA CIEGA

To Santa Cruz del Norte

Location Map

GUANABO

Vía Blanca

WESTERN CUBA

Western Cuba is richly blessed with natural attractions. In Viñales, pincushion buttes - some hiding immense green holes which can only be reached by traipsing through natural corridors - rise steeply over colonial towns, tobacco fields, and forests endowed with endemic flora and fauna. On the southern coast of Matanzas Province lie placid beaches, lagoons, vast swampy marshes and the Bay of Pigs, scene of the 1961 invasion by Cuban exiles who set out to topple Castro's regime.

No less important are the touristy resorts of Isla de la Juventud and Cayo Largo or the beguiling beaches of Varadero, exploited so effectively by Graham Greene as a backdrop in his classic novel *Our Man in Havana*. Here are some of Cuba's ritziest hotels and facilities, with ample opportunities for swimming and diving.

Pinar del Río Province

Tree-covered summits, underground caverns, and limestone promontories eroded into whimsical towers, combine to make Pinar del Río Province one of the most distinctive areas in Cuba. But it is the tobacco plant for which the region is justly famous. Cradled in the small *hoyos* (valleys) of the **Vuelta Abajo**, south-west of Pinar del Río City, are lush seas of tobacco plantations which give the province its wealth. Most of the tobacco grown here is reserved for the production and sale of export cigars, which also provides a major source of income for the economy as well as the main prestige product from the island.

Because of the rampantly fertile soils, other crops such as sugar, citrus fruits and vegetables are also produced in abundance.

Pinar Del Río City

The provincial capital, Pinar del Río City (population 130,000) is a rambling city of neoclassical villas and faded, wooden houses. Founded in 1774, it was named after a thicket of pine trees lining the banks of the Río Guamá.

The city has none of the loveliness of rural Pinar del Río which means travellers generally only hang around for a day.

How to get there

By Rail
Trains run every other day from Havana for $6.50.

By Car
Pinar del Río City is an uneventful 176km drive west from Havana. The six-lane Autopista Nacional ('National Highway') extends from Havana and finishes just before the entrance to the city.

Accommodation
Pinar del Río, Calle Martí y Autopista, ph 5070 - 136 rooms, Soviet-style architecture, a statue in the grounds would make stout old Cortés turn in his grave, comfortable without being special, shop, nightclub, pool - $32.

Entertainment
The city has little in the way of nightspots apart from a nightclub in the Pinar del Río Hotel and the *Rumayor*, a restaurant-cum-cabaret in the northern outskirts. The food is affordable and tasty - mainly rice, beans and chicken - and there's often a karaoke-style live act or dancing to follow. All the city's bars and hotels serve a drink called *La Guayabita del Pinar*, made from guava, rum and spices. Very tasty.

Sightseeing
The pick of the city's attractions is the **Natural History Museum** at Calle José Martí No 202. Housed in a former mansion of wonderfully discordant design - part Greek temple, part Gothic nightmare - the museum has exhibits largely devoted to wildlife once endemic to the province. Admission is $1. Further west, on the same street, is the **Historical Museum**, where the focus is on local history and the violinist Enrique Jorrín, inventor of the cha-cha-cha. The city also has a small **tobacco museum**, on Calle Máximo Gómez, which explains the cigar-making process in minute detail. It's a friendly fug of toxicity and well worth a visit.

NOTES

Vuelta Abajo

About 20km west of the city, around the towns of **San Juan y Martínez** and **San Luis,** is the Vuelta Abajo. Thanks largely to the delicately fine soils, a subtropical climate and superior methods of cultivation, this region grows some of the world's finest tobacco.

The Big Smoke

Cigars continue to be popular today with the Cohiba (Cuba's premier cigar and the size of a small torpedo) remaining the favoured brand. Those to have succumbed to its allure over the years include Groucho Marx, George Burns, David Letterman, Orson Welles, Madonna, Bill Cosby, Jack Nicholson, Demi Moore, Rudyard Kipling, Somerset Maugham, HL Mencken, George Sand (the first woman to smoke cigars in public), Jean Paul Sartre, Lenin and Winston Churchill, who is reported to have smoked a quarter of a million cigars before his death. Castro, who is thought to have invented the Cohiba, was probably the most famous contemporary cigar smoker until he gave up in 1985 in support of a general health campaign against smoking. Bill Clinton too used to be a smoker; these days, according to his aides, he only chews them.

Of course, history is also peppered with those who said no to a puff including Adolph Hitler, who once inveighed: 'Those who don't smoke, follow me!'.

Viñales

Squatting prettily to the north of Pinar del Río City is the town of Viñales. Designated a national monument, it's a splash of thatched-roofed buildings and yawning, tree-lined streets. Surrounding the town is a striking valley famous for its *mogotes* - isolated, craggy formations topped by trees and greenery dating back to the Jurassic period (150 million years ago). Piercing the mogotes are a number of large caverns, some serving as natural cisterns.

The area's hills also abound with rare cork palm (now considered a botanical treasure with only 2000 specimens found), and the cave-dwelling pygmy boa constrictor.

How to get there

By Road

Viñales is 27km north of Pinar del Río City (take the coastal road) and 188km from Havana. The journey from Havana takes about four hours and winds through sugar and tobacco plantations, and knuckles of thickly wooded hills. A tour from Havana is $39.

Accommodation

Los Jasmines, Carretera de Viñales Km 25, ph 93 265 - 74 rooms, superb location on a cliff with great views over the valley, excellent walks nearby, good restaurant and bar, shops, pool - $25-31.

La Ermita, Carretera a la Ermita Km 2, ph 93 204 - 64 rooms, another superb location and more good walks, above-average food and rooms, pool - $25-31.

Rancho San Vicente, Carretera a Puerto Esperanza Km 38, ph 93 200 - 29 rooms, near the Cuevo del Indio cave, pleasant atmosphere, popular and often full, thermal pool - $23-31.

Eating Out

Valle de Prehistoria - located beneath the Mural de la Prehistoria, serves mainly roast pork (excellent, if gazing up at the mural doesn't give you a nosebleed), very popular with video-burdened tourists.

Cuevo del Indio - close to the cave of the same name, good chicken and stew dishes, popular also.

Sightseeing

About 2km north of Viñales, in the Valle de Dos Hermanas (Two Sisters), is the **Mural de la Prehistoria** (1959-66). Painted on a rocky side of a mogote by Leovigilda González (a pupil of the famous Mexican Diego Rivera), the artwork measures 120 metres in height and 180 metres long, and illustrates the different stages of evolution, from snail through to man.

Several kilometres further north is the **Cueva del Indio**, a giant cave measuring 8km in length. Inside you can travel the cave's length by foot or take a 10-minute boat trip. Admission is $2. As the name implies, the cave was once used by the local Indian population and as a shelter for runaway slaves. Another cave in the area is the **Cueva de los Portales**. Discovered in 1800, it was used as one of the country's main facilities of heath tourism in the 1940s, and in 1962 as a subterranean headquarters for Ché Guevara during the Cuban Missile Crisis. It's now an excellent and very crowded campsite.

Cayo Levisa, a tiny, unspoiled island with a good swimming beach is nearby.

Sorora

Nestled in the foothills of the Sierra del Rosario mountains is Sorora, a woodsy spa and resort. The town is named after Jean Paul Soroa, a French plantation owner who fled the Haitian slave uprising in the late 18th century.

How to get there

By Road

Sorora is 95km from Havana and 81km from Pinar del Río City. From Havana, take the Autopista Nacional which goes most of the way to Pinar del Río City; there's a detour to Soroa just before you reach the city.

Accommodation

Villa Soroa, Carretera Soroa Km 8, ph 2122 - 31 rooms, near the Orchidarium and waterfall, bungalow-style accommodation, close to many walks, noisy bar, pool - $25-32.

Eating Out

Castillo de los Nubes ('Castle in the Clouds') - in an ersatz castle above the Orchidarium, reasonable chicken and fish dishes, fusty atmosphere.

Sightseeing

About 5km after the turn-off to Sorora is the **Orchidarium.** Founded in 1943 by Canary Islander Tomás Camacho, these fecund gardens contain over 700 species of orchid (250 of which are endemic) as well as other flowering plants. Admission is $2.

Immediately below the gardens is a carpark and a pathway that leads down to the **El Salto Cascades.** The waterfall here (admission $1), enclosed by a multitude of vegetation, is small and postcard perfect.

Guanahacabibes Peninsula National Park

At the westernmost tip of Pinar del Río Province is the flat-land area of Guanahacabibes Peninsula National Park. Recently declared a UNESCO Biosphere Reserve, it is one of Cuba's largest wilderness areas, brimming with native plant and animal life. The peninsula was the final refuge of the island's Indian population following colonisation; archaeological digs frequently unearth vestiges of their settlements in the area.

South of the peninsula is the **Bahía de Corrientes**, which includes the remote resort of **Playa María la Gorda**. According to legend, María la Gorda ('Fat Mary') was a Venezuelan barmaid who was kidnapped by pirates and abandoned at the beach after a shipwreck. Alone and destitute, she made do by selling water (and one is led to believe, her body) to local fishermen and sailors. Apparently, her daily baths at a place known as *Las Tetas de María la Gorda* ('Fat Mary's Breasts') were a real extravaganza. She died, considerably fatter, on the beach many years later. Despite a number of searches, her grave has yet to be found.

The conditions for diving and swimming are excellent (although those without strong swimming skills should be aware that in some places, the bottom dips quite steeply close to the shore).

Matanzas Province

Matanzas (the name means 'slaughter') is just east of Havana Province and takes its name from the provincial capital on the north coast. Legend has it that the city adopted its name after passengers fleeing a shipwreck were hacked to death by Indians; only a few survived, including a woman, who became the property of the chief.

From such sanguinary beginnings, Matanzas Province has prospered. Once the sugarcane capital of Cuba and the home of artists and writers, its now mobbed by visitors wearing hibiscusy shirts, with most attracted to the beaches of Varadero.

Matanzas City

An industrial city with a seaweed-clogged bay, Matanzas was founded in 1693 between the Yumurí and San Juan rivers. Over the years it's been known under a raft of names - the City of Bridges, the City of Rivers and the Athens of Cuba - none of them deserving. It is, though, the birthplace of the rumba and the site where the sport of baseball was first introduced to Cuba. The city's literary pretensions are kept alive by the fact that two of the country's best poets, Carilda Oliver Labra and José Jacinto Milanés, live here.

How to get there

By Rail

There are four trains daily, on the old Hershey Railway (built by the giant US confectionery company), from Havana for less than two centavos.

By Road

Matanzas City is 101km from Havana. The Vía Blanca links the capital through to the city (hitchers are a common sight along this stretch); en route you pass a number of small oil derricks and the photogenic Valle de Yumurí. Tour buses usually make a 20-minute refreshment stop at a massive bridge overlooking the valley.

Sightseeing

Matanzas has a few sights of note including the splendidly restored **Teatro Sauto**, on **Vigía Square**. Built in 1863, this three-tiered theatre has attracted a bevy of international stars including Sarah Bernhardt and the dancer Ana Pavlova. Admission is $1. A short walk east, on the corner of calles Milanés and Jovellanos, is the **Catedral de San Carlos** (1730), the city's oldest church. Further east is the shady **Parque Libertad**, where locals spend their afternoons fanning themselves with ration books, and the fascinating **Pharmaceutical Museum** (1882). Inside is a large display of apothecary jars and instruments used at the turn of the century. It's open Monday to Saturday from 1-6pm, and 7-10pm.

Five kilometres west of Matanzas City are the **Bellamar Caves**, reputed to be the oldest tourist attraction in Cuba. Discovered in 1861, the caves are a capacious labyrinth of karst crystal formations and dramatic stalagmites and stalactites. Many of the formations are named for some fanciful resemblance - Ladies Salon, Tunnel of Love, the Carrot Garden, and so on. Admission is $2.

Varadero

Built on a 20km finger of sand, Varadero or *La Playa Azúl* ('The Blue Beach') derives its name from a Spanish farming community that took root here in the late 18th century. Since the 1930s when US industrialist Irénée Du Pont built an estate then bought and sold property to wealthy Americans, Varadero has been a boomtown, and is today the jewel in Cuba's tourist crown.

Massive development and an influx of foreign currency have given rise to outcrops of luxury hotels, villas and shopping plazas, with yachts and cruisers clogging the canals. Interspersed among the glass and steel are dilapidated weatherboard houses, lending Varadero that faintly seedy, seaside feel.

By day, the resort's laidback atmosphere is interrupted only by the shrill of two-stroke engines, the blast of tour bus horns and the cries of *'Mira! Mira!'* ('Look! Look!') by the bored *jiniteras*. But at night, everybody puts on their best clothes and goes trolling for action.

How to get there

By Air

Flights leave regularly from Havana for $20 (one way). There are flights also from Canada and Jamaica. Varaderos airport is the Juan Gualberto Gomez International Airport, west of the city. A taxi from the airport to the city centre is $14.

Airline offices at the airport include *Cubana*, ph 63 016, and *Aerocarribean*, ph 70 4965.

By Road

Varadero is a 140km, two-hour drive from Havana. The Vía Blanca highway continues west from Matanzas City all the way to Varadero, where it veers left over a bridge into the city centre. If money is no barrier, you can hire a taxi from Havana for around $75. The best and quickest option is to travel from Havana by luxury tour bus for $27. Varaderos bus station is on the corner of Autopista Sur and Calle 36; the wait for tickets takes days.

Tourist Information

Tourist offices include: *Cubatur*, Ave Primera No 3206; *Cubalse*, cnr Ave Primera and Calle 31; *Havanatur*, cnr Ave Primera and Calle 31 (across the road from the Cubalse office); *Assistur*, Calle 3I No 101.

Money can be changed at the Banco Financiero International on Ave

Playa between calles 32 and 32C, and international calls can be made from the telephone office on the corner of Ave Primera and Calle 64. There are Photoservice branches at Centro Commercial Copey, Calle 63, and on the corner of Ave Playa and Calle 44. A police station is on the corner of Ave Primera and Calle 39.

Accommodation

The prices for the following hotels are high season and doubles only:

Meliá Varadero, Autopista Sur, Playa de Las Américas, ph 66 220 - 497 rooms, close to the former Du Pont estate and the city's golf course, massive lobby the size of an aeroplane hangar, atrium, excellent restaurants and bars (though the wave-crashing music may soon pall), good facilities for children, gym, nightclub, good pool - $160.

Paradiso-Puntarena, Final de Kawama, ph 63 917 - 518 rooms, newish, twin facilities, for the price it could be a lot better, pool - $145.

Internacional, Ave Las Américas, ph 63 011 - 165 rooms, Art Deco design, hotel and bungalow-style accommodation, pleasant atmosphere, excellent nightclub and cabaret, good shops, two tennis courts, saltwater pool - $145.

Cuatro Palmas, Ave Primera e/ 61 y 62, ph 63 912 - 222 rooms, hotel and two-storey bungalow-style accommodation, good recreational facilities and daily activities, close to shopping complex, pool - $120.

Acuazul, Ave Primera e/ 13 y 14, ph 63 918 - 156 rooms, pool - $65.

Villa Punta Blanca, Kawama Final, ph 63 916 - 320 rooms, freshwater and salt-water pools - $60.

Herradura, Ave Playa e/ 35 y 36, ph 63 703 - 79 rooms, comfortable - $50.

Varazul, Ave Primera e/ 14 y 15, ph 63 918 - 69 rooms, quiet - $40.

Caribe, cnr Ave Playa and Calle 30, ph 63 310 - 124 rooms, popular, pool - $40.

Villa Sotavento, Calle 14 e/ Ave Primera y Camino del Mar, ph 63 918 - 130 rooms, clean, good value, pool - $38.

Los Delfines, cnr Ave Playa and Calle 39, ph 63 815 - 38 rooms, close to beach - $35.

Pullman, Calle 49 No 4904 y Ave Primera, ph 62 575 -15 rooms, outstanding value, budget favourite, great atmosphere, good views of the main street, excellent food prepared by one of Varadero's best chefs, very friendly staff and service, small gazebo bar - $32.

Local Transport

Car

Car rental companies include: *Havanautos,* ph 33 7094; Gaviota, ph 33 7240; *Transauto,* ph 33 7336.
Petrol can be bought at Autopista Sur y Calle 17 and Vía Blanca Km 131, La Darsena.

Taxi

Taxis in Varadero are among the most expensive in Cuba - a ride along Ave Primera, Varaderos main street, will cost at least $7. Service can be requested by calling the following: *Cubanacán,* ph 33 7089; *Cubataxi,* ph 63674; *Turistaxi,* ph 63733; *Veracuba,* ph 63377.

Motorbike

Mopeds can be rented from hotels and a number of sidewalk stands on Ave Primera. Prices start at $9 for one hour, $12 for two hours and $15 for three hours.

Bicycle

Bicycles can be rented at hotels including the Villa Caleta, cnr Ave Primera and Calle 19, for around $3-5 an hour.

Eating Out

Most hotels and villas dish up expensive Western-style food and good seafood buffets. Fast food is sold at stalls and cafés along Ave Primera and also by hawkers on the beach. Cheap rolls, breadsticks and pastries can be bought from a bakery on the corner of Ave Primera and Calle 43. Restaurants include:

Casa de Antiguedades, Ave Primera e/ 56 y 59, ph 62 044 - open 4-11pm - international cuisine.

Coppelia, Calle 46 (towards the beach) - as always, the best ice-cream around.

El Bodegón Criollo, cnr Ave Playa and Calle 40, ph 62 180 - open noon-1am - charming atmosphere with the odd strolling guitarist, very popular, Cuban food.

El Meson del Quijote, Carretera Las Américas, ph 63 522 - open 3-11pm - good seating, Spanish food, quite pricey.

La Cabañita, cnr Camino del Mar and Calle 9, ph 62 215 - open 7pm-1am - steak and fish dishes.

Lai Lai, cnr Ave Primera and Calle 18, ph 63 297 - open 7pm-1am - Chinese food.

Las Américas, Carretera Las Américas, ph 66 162 - open noon-11pm - located in the former Du Pont estate, steak and lobster, average bar at the top of the restaurant with good views, could blow your entire budget.

Mediterraneo, cnr Ave Primera and Calle 54, ph 62 460 - open 11.30am-11.45pm - Cuban food.

Mi Casita, Camino del Mar e/ 11 y 12, ph 63 787 - open 7pm-1am - delicious lobster.

Retiro Josone, Ave Primera e/ 56 y 59, ph 62 740 - open noon-11pm - international cuisine.

Entertainment

Varadero's main cinema is the *Cine Varadero*, Ave Playa e/ 42 y 43. All the larger hotels have bars and nightclubs but if you want a change of setting, try the busy *Bavaria Bar*, cnr of Ave Primera and Calle 13. Other popular nightspots include the *Havana Club Discotheque*, cnr Ave Resort 2da and Calle 64 (admission $10), the average Joe's hangout for tawdry romance, and the *Anfiteatro*, cnr of Vía Blanca and Carretera de Cárdenas, which has a lively cabaret.

The best and most popular time to visit Varadero is during the *Carnival* (January 9-February 3). 'Kings' and 'Queens' chosen from different hotels preside over events which include picnics, rum-drinking contests, conga lines, formal parades and a golf tournament. If you're shy, beware - audience participation is vigorously encouraged.

Calle Heredia, Santiago de Cuba.

Shopping

Flanking Ave Primera are handicraft and souvenir stalls; shopping complexes bursting with expensive clothing, cigars and alcohol; fashion boutiques; bookshops stocking English-language airport novels and two-week-old copies of *Time* and *Newsweek*; art galleries with good selections of ceramics; dollar stores; and flimsy lean-tos selling refreshments and cigarettes. *Artex* has a branch on Ave Primera e/ 46 y 47 and another on Calle 60, towards the Atabey Hotel. There is also a branch of *Video Centro* on the corner of Ave Primera and Calle 44.

Sightseeing

What's to see when all before you is crystal-clear waters and endless, white-sand beaches? Not much, quite frankly. The **Parque Josone**, at the eastern end of Ave Primera, is an evergreen enclosure with fountains, miniature lake and island, cafés and a shopping mall. If you're clapped out from partying the night before, **horse-drawn** carriages can be rented outside the main gates for around $3 an hour. Further east, through an area of red-stuccoed bungalows, is Du Pont's former estate - immodestly called **Xanadu** - which is now an overpriced restaurant. And that's about it, unless the sight of families wheeling old b&w TVs down the street or foreigners kerb-crawling for *jiniteras* count as attractions.

Tours

Excursions can be booked at any major hotel or at tourist offices. On offer are two-day tours to Pinar del Río Province ($105), one-day visits to the ramshackle colonial town of Cárdenas (where the Cuban flag was first flown in 1850) and, further south, Laguna del Tesoro (site of a crocodile breeding farm - reptiles one day, handbags the next - and the resort of Guamá) $33; helicopter rides over Varadero and Matanzas Province; and stopovers at a number of Caribbean destinations including Cancún, Caracas, Nassau and Montego Bay.

Sport and Recreation

Marinas Gaviota (at Varadero's eastern tip), Acua and Chapelín, as well as most hotels, can arrange helicopter and light aircraft rides, yacht cruises, equipment and guides for fishing, scuba diving, water skiing, kayaks, catamarans, sail and rowing boats, as well as tennis, shooting, archery, volleyball, badminton and horseback rides. The list of activities is endless (and exhausting, which is why so many give up and spend their time lazing in the sun).

For tennis, the Marina Gaviota and Atabey, Varadero International, Varazul and Sol Palmeras hotels have courts. Golfers, pack your plus-fours - Varadero, at the time of writing, was undergoing construction of the largest 18-hole golf course in the country with the erstwhile Du Pont mansion being pencilled in as the location of the new clubhouse. Green fees at the present nine-hole course, near the Las Américas Restaurant, are $10 for one round and $15 for two rounds. Golf club hire is $10.

There's also a diving centre on Calle 24, towards the beach. That mainstay of the seaside - the mini golf course - can be found at the Sol Palmeras Hotel and at Ave Primera between calles 41 and 42.

Zapata Peninsula

Just over 100km south of Varadero is the Zapata Peninsula, an enormous natural reserve rich in native marine and birdlife. Once feared for its legion of crocodiles, the swampy marshes are now haven to bee hummingbirds, manatees, tarpon, largemouth bass and the rare *manjuarí* (which looks like a cross between an alligator and a fish). This lacustrine paradise also abounds in *cenotes* (limestone sinkholes flooded with rainwater), which are part of one of the largest lake and cave systems in Latin America.

To the south west, on the shimmering **Laguna del Tesoro** ('Treasure Lake'), is the resort of **Guamá**. A reconstructed Indian village built on a series of islands, all interlinked by wooden bridges, means it is often described as the 'Venice of the Americas'. The majority of visitors are foreign anglers who come here to catch largemouth bass. Apart from their rods and tackle, they also bring insect repellent - the mosquitos are vicious.

Further south is **Playa Larga**, on the deep-water **Bahía de Cochinos** ('Bay Of Pigs'). It's a small, pretty ribbon of sand and an excellent base for treks to bird-watching stations. Lying on the south-eastern shores of the bay is **Playa Girón**. In the early part of the 17th century, this stretch of beach gained infamy as the haunt of pirates and corsairs, but it's now better known as the site of the thwarted 1961 invasion by US-trained Cuban mercenaries.

The diving here is excellent but is recommended only for expert divers.

Accommodation

Villa Guamá, Laguna del Tesoro, ph 2979 - 50 rooms, thatched-roof cabins, folksy but run-down, pool - $20-25.

Villa Paya Girón, Playa Girón, ph 4110 - 255 rooms, reasonable facilities, close to dive sites, tennis court, pool - $19-25.

Sightseeing

The lead-up and suppression of the 1961 Bay of Pigs landing is documented in extraordinary detail at the **Museo Playa Girón**, at the beach of the same name. After leaving the museum, the landscape suddenly appears jungly, full of ideal spots for an ambush

Isla de la Juventud

Isla de la Juventud ('Island of Youth') is the largest island (3000 sq km) in the Archipielago de los Canarreos, and lies 138km south of Havana and 97km from the mainland. Discovered by Columbus in 1494 (who called it 'La Evangelista'), the island has been many things over the years: a hiding place for pirates and the supposed inspiration for Robert Louis Stevenson's novel *Treasure Island*; an island protectorate of the USA; a grim penal colony for Cuban revolutionaries; a seat of learning for international students (formerly known as the Isle of Pines, the island was renamed in 1978 because of this new role); and today, a special municipality that is an important citrus, ceramic and marble-producing area as well as a major tourist destination.

Hart Crane

Hart Crane, the noted US poet and notoriously heavy drinker, first came to the Isla de la Juventud as a starry-eyed 17-year-old in 1916. He visited several times, usually staying at his grandfather's citrus farm, where he would spend his time writing letters and the occasional poem. In 1932, Crane left the island for the USA. Unfortunately, he never arrived - once the boat had moved far enough from shore, he jumped overboard to disappear forever.

Much of the island's population (70,000) is found in the agriculturally rich north, while the south, with its limestone soils, has a lightly populated acreage, and is covered with swampy marshes and dense patches of woodlands.

How to get there

By Air

Cubana has five weekly flights from Havana for $17 (one way). Isla de la Juventuds airport is 15km south of Nueva Gerona.

By Sea

Daily passenger and transport ferries leave from the port of Batabanó, on Cuba's southern coast.

Accommodation

El Colony, Carretera de Siguanea Km 16, ph 98 181 - 83 rooms, remote location on the island's south-west coast, hotel and bungalow-style accommodation, recently refurbished, good bar, dive shop and practice pool, close to dive sites, very popular - $55-70.

Eating Out

El Cochinito, Calle 39, Nueva Gerona - hardly a standout, typical Cuban fare consisting of cheap pork and fish dishes.

Coppelia, Calle 37 e/ 30 y 32, Nueva Gerona.

Shopping

Isla de la Juventud is Cuba's largest producer of ceramics. Much of what is made here is tacky and uninteresting (ashtrays, vases, etc), but the brightly coloured *ceramitas* (relief-designed tiles) are exceptionally good value. The most popular decorations usually have a nautical or floral theme.

Sightseeing

Nueva Gerona (population 14,000), the island's capital, has a tiny museum and square but very little in the way of attractions. Probably the only highlight is the **El Pinero**, the boat Castro took to Mexico when he was pardoned by Batista. It can be found near the Batabanó ferry landing. A half-hour drive north-west of town is the **Playa Bibijagua**, a black-sand beach that looks less than inviting.

About 4km south-west of Nueva Gerona is the **El Abra Farm**, the place where a youthful José Martí was sent before he was exiled to Spain. The farmhouse is now a museum containing a small collection of Martí memorabilia.

The **Model Prison**, an enormous penitentiary built to accommodate over 6000 inmates, is just east of town. This is where Castro and his brother were confined following the Moncada barracks attack in 1953. For Castro, it proved an especially productive time: he read widely (pouring continuously over the works of Martí), corresponded with supporters on the mainland, studied and kept fit, and dreamt that one day he 'would rise from the ashes like a phoenix'. He was released in 1955 and moved to Mexico. The rest, as they say, is history. You can relive his formative years at the prison by visiting a museum, housed in the former hospital wing.

At the south-eastern extreme of the island are the **Punta del Este Caves**, a chain of seven caverns holding a wealth of early Indian *petroglyphs* (rock paintings). The main cave has over 200 pictographs alone. Discovered by the shipwrecked French sailor Freeman P Lane in 1910, they are considered the most important of their kind in the Antilles Archipelago.

Sport and Recreation

Isla de la Juventud has some of the best diving in the world with over 50 dive sites including **Punta el Cayuelo**, on the island's south-western tip, and the **Costa de los Piratas**, in the south-east. The latter is a protected area and has a number of features such as cliff walls, channels, caves, coralline formations and a myriad of marine life. Treasure hunts - for amounts of $5000 or more - are often held in late May and attract divers from around the world. Albert Falco, captain of the famous research ship *Calypso*, is a regular visitor.

Equipment can be hired at the *El Colony Hotel*, which is also the headquarters of the International Diving Centre.

Cayo Largo

Lying in the eastern corner of the Archipielago de los Canarreos, Cayo Largo is one of the most westernised resorts in Cuba. It has great beaches, plenty of water activities and lots of nattily dressed, well-groomed, narcissistic tourists

How to get there

By Air

Aerocarribean has regular half-hour flights from Havana ($37.50 one way) as well as Isla de la Juventud, Varadero, Cienfuegos and Santiago de Cuba. There are also charter flights from Europe, Canada and Grand Cayman. A tour from Havana is $94.

Opposite Museo
Municipal de
Historia, Trinidad

CIENFUEGOS CITY

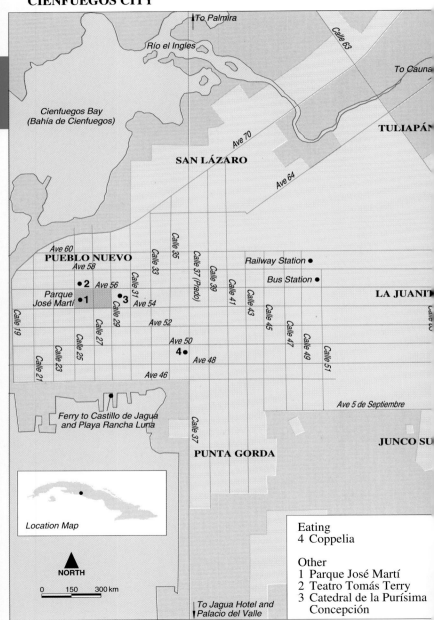

To Palmira

Río el Ingles

Calle 63

To Cauna

Cienfuegos Bay
(Bahía de Cienfuegos)

Ave 70

TULIAPÁN

SAN LÁZARO

Ave 64

Ave 60

PUEBLO NUEVO

Ave 58

Calle 35

Calle 37 (Prado)

Calle 39

Railway Station ●

Bus Station ●

LA JUANI

● 2 Ave 56

Calle 31

Calle 41

Calle 43

Parque
José Martí ● 1

● 3 Ave 54

Calle 33

Calle 45

Calle 47

Calle 49

Calle 19

Calle 27

Calle 29

Ave 52

Calle 51

Calle 25

Ave 50

4 ● Ave 48

Calle 23

Calle 21

Ave 46

Ferry to Castillo de Jagua
and Playa Rancha Luna

Calle 37

Ave 5 de Septiembre

JUNCO SU

PUNTA GORDA

Location Map

NORTH

0   150   300 km

To Jagua Hotel and
Palacio del Valle

Eating
4 Coppelia

Other
1 Parque José Martí
2 Teatro Tomás Terry
3 Catedral de la Purísima
  Concepción

Accommodation

The prices for the following hotels (all have air-conditioning, cable TV, sporting equipment hire, etc) are high season.

Pelícano, ph 79 4215 - 236 rooms - saltwater pool - $135.

Isla del Sur, ph 79 4215 - 59 rooms - saltwater pool - $125.

Villa Capricho, ph 79 4215 - 60 rooms - bungalow-style accommodation, right on the beach - $120.

Villa Coral, ph 79 4215 - 66 rooms - bungalow-style accommodation, good views, saltwater pool - $120.

Villa Iguana, ph 79 4215 - 118 rooms - Spanish-style, two-storey stucco accommodation, saltwater pool - $80.

Eating Out

Hotels on the island all have restaurants which serve expensive seafood buffets (lots of lobster salad), pasta and pizza.

Tours

Day-trips are available to the heavily-fished waters of Cayo Rico, west of Cayo Largo, for $40. Other excursions go to the secluded Cayo Cantiles, the lizard-filled Cayo Iguana, and Cayo Pajaros, a migratory stop for seabirds.

Sport and Recreation

Cayo Largo offers lots of water activities including sailing, snorkelling, windsurfing, fishing, etc. The Sambo Head shallows, west of Cayo Largo, is a popular dive site laden with sunken ships and their remnants. Hotels and local services can rent watersports equipment as well as cars, bicycles, horses and even a plane if you're really bored.

The islands western beaches include the placid **Playa Sirena**, which is the best swimming and snorkelling beach but is often crowded, and **Playa Lindamar**, which is smaller and more private. The island's midriff is dominated by **Playa Blanca** while **Playa Tortuga**, at the eastern tip, is an important wildlife habitat.

NOTES

CENTRAL CUBA

Most travellers tend to give Central Cuba a wide berth, preferring instead the jazzed-up comforts of Havana and Vardero, or the iconic eastern city of Santiago de Cuba. Which is a pity, as it is an area with a rich heritage. Three of the country's first settlements are here including the charming, colourfully decorated city of Camagüey. Attracting the greatest knot of onlookers, though, is Trinidad. With its lovingly tended colonial buildings and seesawing history of 16th-century *conquistadors*, 17th-century *corsairs* and 18th-century sugar barons, it is a must see for any visitor to the country.

There's also the seaside city of Cienfuegos, embracing one of Cuba's most beautiful bays and a host of activities including trekking and wildlife excursions in Sancti Spíritus Province, fishing at Lake Hanabanilla and Laguna de la Leche, diving among wrecks off the north-eastern coast and swimming in the southern archipelago. *Vaqueros* (cowboys), trotting along on horseback or pulling teams of donkeys and oxen, are a common sight in the central plains, as are flocks of pink flamingos along the northern beaches.

Cienfuegos Province

Lying on the southern coast of Central Cuba, Cienfuegos Province was a former site of Indian settlements and a popular haunt of pirates and corsairs. Until recently it has been predominantly agricultural, but massive development - including the construction of oil refineries and a nuclear power station (since stalled) - has now made it one of the most industrialised provinces in the country.

The broad, well laid-out city of Cienfuegos, which sits on a picturesque harbour, is the main attraction for visitors.

Cienfuegos City

The provincial capital, Cienfuegos City (population 107,000) was founded on the luminous, crescent-shaped Jagua Bay in 1819 by French settlers from Bordeaux. They originally called the city Fernandina de Jagua, but hastily renamed it in honour of the then Spanish captain-general Don José Cienfuegos (who had been instrumental in their arrival). Today the 'Pearl of the South', as it is commonly known, is a bright, attractive seaport with colonial palaces, gracious streets and parks, a wide central esplanade that extends all the way to the end of the peninsula, and an excellent beach.

How to get there

By Rail

Trains run three times weekly from Havana for $11. The railway station is on Ave 60, east of the city.

By Road

Cienfuegos City is 336km from Havana. To get to Cienfuegoes, take the Autopista Nacional until you see a signpost to the city; from here its a one-hour drive away along a narrow road. A two-day tour from Havana is $109. The bus station is on Ave 56, a block south of the railway station.

Accommodation

Jagua, Calle 37 No 1, Punta Gorda, ph 6362 - 154 rooms, overlooking Jagua Bay and next to the Palacio del Valle restaurant, nice decor, inexpensive snack bar, good nightclub, saltwater pool - $36-45.

Pasacaballo, Carretera Rancho Luna Km 22, ph (09) 6212 - 204 rooms, out of town, popular with Cubans, pool - $29-35.

Rancho Luna, Carretera Rancho Luna Km 16, ph (04) 8120 - 237 rooms, another out of town hotel, good views overlooking the entrance to the bay, close to swimming beaches and dive sites, plenty of sports activities including tennis, badminton and volleyball, windsurfing and scuba-diving lessons, gardens, beach bar, organises tours in and around Cienfuegos, pool - $25-31.

Local Transport

There's a paucity of transport options in the city although daily ferries regularly depart from a pier at the end of Calle 29 to both Playa Rancha Luna and Castillo de Jagua. Otherwise you'll have to hoof it.

Eating Out

Palacio del Valle, behind the Jagua Hotel - expensive and ordinary food but the setting - in a Moorish-style building right on the bay - is delightful; *La Verja*, Calle 54 - big helpings of steak, omelettes and lobster, good location in a former colonial mansion, quite pricey; *Coppelia*, Calle 37 e/ 48 y 50.

Sightseeing

The city's major artery is **Calle 37**, better known as the Prado. Reminiscent of its namesake in Havana with its oak trees and benches, the Prado is a prime meeting place for the inhabitants of the city. Another focal point for *cienfuganos* is the **Parque José Martí**, on Calle 54, which is surrounded by colonial mansions and neoclassical buildings built in the 19th and early 20th century. Declared a national monument, the park is dominated by a white-marble statue of Martí, guarded by a pair of playful-looking lions. To one end a triumphal arch commemorates the founding of the Cuban Republic in 1902.

The three-storey **Teatro Tomás Terry** (1890), named after a rich plantation owner, is just north of the park. This theatre, which once played host to Caruso and the like, has been extensively refurbished and features good ceiling frescoes above the orchestra pit. East of the park, across Calle 29, is the mustard-coloured **Catedral de la Purísima Concepción**. Built in 1819, its collection of stained-glass windows representing the 12 Apostles is considered the loveliest in all of Cuba's churches.

South along the Prado, opposite the Jagua Hotel, is the **Palacio del Valle**. An exotic concoction of Gothic, Venetian and mostly Moorish architecture, the house was bought by Alejandro Suero Balbin and given to his daughter as a wedding present. Today it's home to a souvenir store and the city's best restaurant.

Some 20km east of the city is **Playa Rancha Luna**, a good black-sand beach and resort close to several dive sites. Also in the vicinity is the **Castillo de Jagua** (1732-45), the city's oldest structure, which was originally built to stymie smuggling between the townspeople and English pirates. It was later strengthened following the Spanish attack on English ships during the War of Jenkins Ear. Legend has it that every night a blackbird would circle the small fort and then turn into the 'Blue Lady', who would stalk the rooms and corridors scaring the bejabbers out of the sleeping soldiers. No one wanted to stand guard, but one night, a soldier gamely accepted. The following morning he was found - collapsed in fear though still clutching his sword - strewn with pieces of blue cloth from the lady's dress. The hapless fellow subsequently spent the rest of his life in an asylum.

Further east, in the serene spot of Soledad, is the **Botanical Gardens** (9 sq km). Founded in 1901 by Harvard University, it is the repository for a remarkable array of butterfly jasmine, cacti and other plants indigenous to the island.

Vila Clara Province

Often overlooked by travellers, Vila Clara Province summons up enough sights to make a leisurely visit worthwhile. Much of the countryside is dotted with sugar plantations, tobacco fields and brick houses with striking red-tiled roofs, while the university city of Santa Clara is the site of a decisive battle between rebels and Batista's forces prior to the Revolution.

Santa Clara

The provincial capital, Santa Clara (population 182,000) was founded in 1689 after a group of families from the town of Remedios - withering under constant attack by pirates - were forced to move inland. The peace and quiet those first settlers so hankered for is much in evidence today as students dawdle to classrooms and old timers snooze to the lulling sounds of birds in the main square. The only hint of activity comes from the large INPUD factory, opened by Ché Guevara in 1964, which churns out the odd refrigerator and oven.

How to get there

By Train
Trains run daily from Havana.

Accommodation

Motel Los Caneyes, Carretera de los Caneyes e/ Ave Eucaliptos y Circunvalacion, ph 4512 - 90 rooms, outside the city, apparently designed to look like an Indian village with circular wooden huts, hot showers, cheap food, good services, quiet, pool - $25-31.

Santa Clara Libre, Parque Vidal No 6, ph 7540 - 161 rooms, central location, reasonable value - $21-24.

Elguea, Corralillo, ph 6240 - 105 rooms, at the spa of the same name, north-west of Santa Clara, close to thermal pools, physiotherapy room, sporting facilities, pool - $20-23.

Sightseeing

The city's main square is the leafy **Parque Vidal**, named after Leoncio Vidal, a Cuban independence fighter who was killed in 1898. At the northern corner of the square is the **Teatro de la Caridad**, a munificent gift of Marta Abreu de Estevez to the city in memory of her parents.

The **Museum of Decorative Arts**, filled with antique furnishings and knick-knackery, is nearby.

North-east of the square, across a bridge, is the **Tren Blidado**, Santa Clara's most important attraction. On 28 December 1958, rebel guerillas derailed a train loaded with government soldiers and weapons as it left for the Sierra Maestra. Fierce fighting broke out over the city and by the evening of 31 December, the rebels had won a resounding victory. For Batista, who was fully aware of his army's inept performances, this was the last straw - he fled at dawn the next day for exile in the Dominican Republic. Several carriages have now been preserved and house exhibits of the attack.

Those epochryphal three days are again expressed in the architecture of the **Plaza de la Revolución**, south-west of the square - another of Cuba's grandiose formal spaces and another with a statue of Ché Guevara in the centre.

Lake Hanabanilla

A short drive south of Santa Clara, through sugar plantations and the thickly wooded hills of the Escambray Mountains, is the man-made Lake Hanabanilla (36 sq km). Created by a hydro-electric power plant that supplies energy to the region, the reservoir is renowned as one of the best spots for snaring largemouth bass (which were brought into Cuba in 1928 from Texas and New Orleans) in the world. Girding the lakes shores are a few patchy farms and the Hanabanilla Hotel, which organises day-trips into the surrounding mountains, rents out boats and provides fishing equipment.

Accommodation

Hanabanilla, Manicaragua, ph 49 125 - 126 rooms, Soviet-style architecture, on the shores of the lake, close to nearby walks, fishing and hiking services, pool - $33-41.

Remedos

Founded in 1524 by a Spanish farmer, Remedios (population 17,000) is 45km north-east of Santa Clara. In the early 19th century, a fire almost razed the town to the ground - its fine collection of Spanish colonial buildings, squares and houses are testament to what was achieved after that. Little has changed in Remedios since then with bicycles and horse-drawn carts outnumbering vehicles on the town's streets.

Sightseeing

The public focal point of Remedios is **Parque Martí**, which is surrounded by colonial mansions and the city's administrative buildings. Standing on the northern side of the square is the **Caturla Music Museum**, dedicated to the local composer and magistrate Alejandro García Caturla who was slain in 1940. East of the square is the **Iglesia de San Juan Bautista**, an unprepossessing church guarding a gold-encrusted main altar.

The other place of interest in Remedios is the **Museo de las Parrandas**, at Calle Máximo Gómez No 71. The museum is home to a variety of gaudy costumes, fireworks, decorations and floats dedicated to a passionate one-night contest that pits neighbourhood against neighbourhood. Months of preparation and labour precede the Parrandas which was formerly held on the last Saturday before the end of the year, then changed to the last Saturday in July. On the big night, the entire town gathers in Parque Martí to watch the two neighbourhoods try to outdo each other by making the most noise. Obviously, the winner is usually the team with the most stamina and the largest collective pair of tonsils.

Just east of Remedios is the fishing village of **Caibarién**. From here, boats go to **Cayo Conuco**, a popular island with good swimming, walks, and an excellent and cheap hilltop campsite.

Sancti Spíritus Province

Smack in the middle of Cuba is the province of Sancti Spíritus. Its mountains, valleys, beaches, and the fact that it has two of the country's oldest towns, means tourism, rather than a traditional economy based on sugar and tobacco production, now holds sway. Most travellers conveniently forget the province's natural attractions and instead flock to Trinidad, a venerable old relic that is always accompanied by the rubric 'a perfectly preserved colonial city'.

Sancti Spíritus City

One of the first towns to be established on the island, Sancti Spíritus City (population 195,000) was founded by Diego Velázquez in 1514 on the banks of the Río Tuinicú. The city soon flourished, but a vicious plague of biting ants meant settlers were uprooted to its present site on the Río Yayabo eight years later. During the late 16th and 17th centuries, pirates replaced ants as the city's major cause for concern. Today it is a relaxing, utterly unappealing city - the kind of place that when you leave, you no longer remember a blind thing about it.

How to get there

By Train
Trains run daily from Havana for $8.

Accommodation

Vila Rancho Hatuey, Carretara Central Km 383, ph 26 015 - 22 rooms, small and nondescript, also out of town, arranges tours, pool - $29-35.

Zaza, Finca José, Zaza, ph 26 012 - 128 rooms, out of town, good food though indifferent service, close to lake, tennis courts, fishing equipment hire, pool - $23-25.

Sightseeing

The city's main square is the **Parque Central**. A block south-east, on Calle Placido, is the **Iglesia Mayor**, reputed to be the oldest church in Cuba. First built in 1536 out of wood, it was subsequently destroyed after numerous pirate raids and then rebuilt, using more permanent materials such as brick and stone, between 1671-80. The impressive dome was added in the 19th century.

About 5km south of the city is the **Zaza Reservoir**, a man-made lake that is one of Cuba's major fishing sites.

Trinidad

In the foothills of the Escambray Mountains, 67km south-west of Sancti Spíritus, dozes the Spanish colonial city of Trinidad (population 40,000). Like Sancti Spíritus, it is one of Cuba's oldest towns, having been founded by Velázquez in 1514 as a staging post for expeditions to the New World (in 1518, Cortés and his fleet set out from here to conquer Mexico). During the 17th and 18th century, Trinidad was repeatedly sacked by pirates but by the early to mid-19th century, the city's coffers - boosted by the earnings from sugar and slaves - were overflowing. The city's wealth proved fleeting, however, and by the turn of the century, Trinidad's stocks had well and truly sunk.

Sugar production still continues today but it is the tourist industry that provides the biggest source of income. Perfectly preserved for over a century, travellers come to marvel at Trinidad's collage of baronial manors and mansions; squat houses with facades of pastel pink, blue, green and yellow with iron grille-work on the windows; cobble-stoned streets that slant strangely toward the middle to drain away rainwater; and the architecture - a mix of neoclassic and baroque with a Moorish twist.

In 1988, UNESCO declared Trinidad a World Heritage Site.

How to get there

By Air

Aerocaribbean has flights from Havana for $27 (one way). Tours from Havana (including return airfare) are $79 for a one-day visit and $119 for an overnight stay.

By Road

Trinidad is 454km from Havana. By car, the city is best reached from either Cienfuegoes or Sancti Spíritus (a one-day tour from the former is $30). Two buses run daily from Santa Clara but getting a ticket is about as straightforward as sprinting through quicksand.

Accommodation

Ancón, Playa Ancón, ph 4011 - 216 rooms, close to beach and dive sites, very big on package tours, good restaurant and snack bar, plenty of facilities, pool - $34-41.

Costa Sur, Playa María Aguilar, ph 2424 - 111 rooms, again close to beach, pool - $25-31.

Motel Las Cuevas, Finca Santa Ana, ph 2324 - 124 rooms, excellent value, easily the pick of Trinidad's accommodation, built on a hill with good views over the city, 15-minute walk to the centre, bungalow-style accommodation, good restaurant, shop, nightclub, pool - $20-25.

There are also campsites at Playa Ancón and La Boca, south-west of Trinidad. Private rooms can be rented in Trinidad from Sergio Castellanos, Calle Piro Guinart No 69, and Carmen Luisa, Calle Maceo No 373 for $10-12 a night.

Eating Out

Colonial Trinidad, Calle Maceo No 55 - Western-style food.

Guamuhaya, cnr calles Martí and Izquiereda - inexpensive food in a elegant setting.

Meson del Regidor, Calle Simón Bolívar No 430 - restaurant and bar, clean, airy and quiet, though travellers often fall prey to locals genially begging for pens and soft drinks.

Entertainment

Casa de la Trova, Calle Jesús Menéndez - free entry, good live Cuban music, boisterous atmosphere.

La Canchánchara, Calle Real No 44 - more live music, yummy cocktails (including *canchánchara*) but very touristy.

Sightseeing

At the centre of the city is the immaculate **Parque Martí**. Hemmed in by a wrought-iron fence and filled with towering royal palms, the square is one of the gayest and most beautiful in Cuba. Bordering it on all sides are impressive museums and galleries, civic buildings, and the former mansions of local colonial society. Standing on the square's north-east corner is the **Iglesia de la Santísima Trinidad** (1884-92), the city's most important church. At the time of writing, both the church and square were in tatters - a French film crew had commandeered the whole area and was busily and noisily trying to recreate the aftermath of a battle.

The **Museo Romantico de Artes Decorativos**, a short hop west of the church at Calle Enchemendia No 52, was originally a mansion built by wealthy slave traders and then supposedly the home of a Count. Inside you can see all the trappings of a high-class Trinidadian household: gleaming marble floors; carved wooden panels; precious porcelain, china and silverware; colonial furniture, sculpture and paintings. The view over the square from an upper floor balcony is equally impressive. Admission is $3. Just south of the square, on Calle Desengano, is the **Museo de Arquitectura Colonial**, which showcases more interior furnishings culled from the great mansions of Trinidad during the 18th and 19th centuries.

The **Museo de la Lucha Contra Bandidos** ('Museum of the Struggle Against Bandits'), housed in a former convent on Calle del Cristo, details the defeat of Cuban counter-revolutionary guerrilas - dubbed 'bandidos' - who were holed up in the Escambray Mountains. More nuisance value than real threat, Castro's army eventually wiped them out in the mid-1960s. Exhibits are similar to those found in Havana's *Museo de la Revolución* with maps, tools, weapons and valedictions to the dead, etc.

South of here, at Calle Simón Bolívar No 423, is the **Museo Municipal de História** (1827-30). Formerly the home of a 19th-century sugar baron, its rooms display permanent collections of colonial furniture, small and large pieces documenting Trinidad's history and development (an enormous church bell, manuscripts and several coats of arms), as well as exhibits on the local sugar industry (sets of stocks used to shackle slaves, etc). There is also a souvenir stall selling clothing, postcards and maps on the ground floor. Another feature of the museum is a wooden staircase that ascends - passing a couple of good but expensive handicraft workshops along the way - to the roof for splendid views over the city and surrounding countryside. Admission is $3.

Other notable mansions-cum-galleries nearby include the **Museo de Arqueologia**, filled with art and artefacts of Cuba's Indian population, and rumoured to be the site of Hernan Cortes's house; and the **Galeria de Arte Universal**, which has prints purloined from a number of Renaissance paintings plus works by local artists.

The sandy beaches and crystalline waters of the **Peninsula de Ancón** are 10km south of Trinidad. Here you'll find the popular beach resorts of **Ancón, Costa Sur** and **La Boca**, all close to a number of dive sites. A taxi from Trinidad will cost around $10-15.

Tours

The Ancón Hotel organises action-packed day-trips to Topes de Collantes (see under that heading later) for $45. You certainly pay for what you get: lunch and drinks; visits to sugar and coffee plantations; swimming at the base of a nauseatingly pretty waterfall; lots of detours to observe the native fauna including the *tocororo*, Cuba's national bird; and, best of all, a hair-raising 4WD trip up a mountainside.

Valle de los Ingenios

East of Trinidad is the Valle de los Ingenios ('Valley of the Sugarmills'), more commonly known as the San Luís Valley. During the mid-19th century, over 50 sugarmills operated here at the peak of Trinidad's sugar boom. One of the sole remaining mills is the 45-metre **Torre de Iznaga** (admission $1), built by a member of the local sugar oligarchy to oversee his slaves working in the outlying fields. According to legend, the plantation owner was so rich that he decided to pave his palace floors with coins instead of tiles. The Spanish authorities were unimpressed with his request but acquiesced only on the condition that the coins would stand on edge (ouch!), otherwise people would be stepping on the Kings face or the national coat of arms. The baron pondered this awhile. In what must have been a rare moment of lucidity, he abandoned his plan and spent the money instead.

You can climb the 138 steps to the top of the tower and experience the same commanding views the baron once had over the area.

The Valle de los Ingenios was recently declared a Heritage Site of Mankind by UNESCO.

Topes de Collantes

North of Trinidad, along a precipitous road that dips and winds its way into the Escambray Mountains, is Topes de Collantes. Built as a tuberculosis sanatorium in 1954, Topes de Collantes became a heavy-handed training ground for teachers after the Revolution (apparently the drop-out rates were high), and then in the 1970s, one of the principal *policlínicos* (health centres) in the country. It continues to provide curative treatment today - although the equipment is no longer state-of-the-art - mostly to high-ranking officials, the elite and international patients. The complex has a multitude of facilities and services including saunas, steam baths, gyms, pools, anti-stress and weight-reduction treatments, hydromassage, physical culture and other body therapies. In fact, every imaginable thing to help you get back into shape.

Tours

Those who aren't at Topes de Collantes for therapeutic reasons, come to nature-watch or hike in the lush, hilly terrain. Hotels and travel agencies in the area can arrange walks to Pico San Juán (1153m), Pico de Potrerillo (932m), the scenic Caburní Falls as well as excursions to Finca Codina, a former coffee plantation, which is now a wildlife retreat. Horseback rides, seafaris and sailing off the coast are also available.

Accommodation

Los Helechos, Escambray, ph 40 117 - 49 rooms, friendly service, arranges group tours, popular, pool - $21-26.

Ciego de Avila Province

Largely flat (it never reaches more than 50m above sea level) and enclosed by islands to the north and south, Ciego de Avila Province was the scene of bloody fighting in the 19th century. During the Ten Years War, the Spanish constructed a series of fortifications known as the *Trocha* ('Path') which divided the island at its two narrowest points - **Morón** on the northern coast and **Júcaro** to the south. Composed of forts and sentry towers, the wall was built to isolate the rebel armies that had gathered in the east. Obstinately determined to seal their advance, the Spanish captain-general Valeriano Weyler later added ditches and fencing, and erected hundreds of dead, bare, silvery palm trunks that stood like totem poles. Seemingly impregnable, the wall was breeched twice by Cuban troops wielding only swords and machetes, first in 1875 and again twenty years later.

Today the province is one of the largest producers of sugar and pineapples in Cuba, with other crops, especially bananas and citrus fruits, playing a major role in the local economy. For most travellers, the only places that warrant interest are the islands off the north coast and the southern archipelago of **Jardines de la Reina**.

Ciego de Avila City

The provincial capital, Ciego de Avila (population 75,000) was established by a small farming settlement in 1538. Its countrified origins still prevail and it remains little more than a large hick town on a permanent siesta. Lethargy appears the city's main vice, which is why most only tarry on their way to fishing spots in the north and diving and snorkelling excursions to the south.

How to get there

By Air

Flights from Havana are $44 (one way).

By Train

Trains run daily from Havana.

Accommodation

Ciego de Avila, Carretera de Ceballos Km 2 1/2, ph 28 013 - 138 rooms, out of town, Soviet-style architecture, good restaurant with cheap and tasty food, nightclub, pool - $31-39.

Sightseeing

Sorry, only kidding.

Jardines de la Reina

In an archipelago south of Ciego de Avila City stretches Jardines de la Reina ('The Queen's Gardens'). It's one of Cuba's more remote destinations and can be reached mainly by taking an organised tour. The archipelago is home to numerous remote keys, protected reefs, undisturbed beaches and dramatic-sounding - Refuge of the Sponges,

Black Coral Forest, etc - dive sites. There's also a huge variety of marine life in the waters including lobsters, turtles, angelfish, sponges and coral.

The tourist desk at the Ciego de Avila Hotel can organise transport to the archipelago; they can also tell you which dive sites are for experienced divers only.

Morón

The town of Morón is 37km north of Ciego de Avila City. There is little to recommend here, other than its importance as a base for travel to the northern islands, and its proximity to two of Cuba's best angling locations: the odd-looking **Laguna de la Leche** ('Milk Lagoon'), so named because of the white-coloured water - the result of wind stirring the lime deposits on the lakes bed - to the north; and the smaller **Laguna Redonda** to the east.

Accommodation

Morón, Ave Tarafa s/n Morón, ph 3901 - 144 rooms, recently refurbished, average food and service, arranges fishing and boating trips - $35-43.

The Northern Islands

A 32-km-long causeway bridges the coast north of Morón to **Cayo Coco** (364 sq km), a rapidly developing island of beautiful white-sand beaches that stretch for some 30km. Famed as a bird sanctuary, the island abounds in bee hummingbirds and Cuban cuckoos, although most nature-watchers come here to see the rare pink flamingos.

Cayo Guillermo (13 sq km) is further west along the causeway. It has more colonies of seabirds and 5km of good beaches protected by a coral reef less than a kilometre off-shore. Apparently Hemingway was a former visitor which means the fishing must be good.

Accommodation

Guitart, Cayo Coco, ph (05) 3202 - 95 rooms, swank hotel catering mostly to package groups, mock Spanish colonial architecture, corny theme bars ('Hemingway Beach Club'), plenty of facilities and activities, sporting and diving equipment, tennis and badminton courts, nightclub, two pools - $60-75.

Villa Cojímar, Cayo Guillermo, ph (05) 3044 - 90 rooms, small, bungalow-style accommodation, good facilities, boat hire, very laidback - $40-50.

Villa Oceano, Cayo Guillermo, ph (05) 3044 - 8 rooms, small and cosy - $30-35.

Villa Flotante, Cayo Guillermo, ph (05) 3044 - 12 rooms, floating villa that looks like it could do with a couple of gallons of paint, quaint but only for the sight-impaired - $25-35.

Camagüey Province

The largest province in the country, Camagüey is characterised by vast, featureless plains of sugarcane, citrus fruits, vegetables and cattle. Surprisingly for an area so rich in agricultural wealth, there is practically no subsoil water, forcing the first settlers to improvise by making *tinajones* - large earthenware pots similar to those used by the Spanish to transport wine from Spain - for collecting rainwater. The *tinajones* quickly became *de rigueur* for any self-respecting homeowner, much like the microwave oven today. According to a hoary local legend, if a woman offers a man water from a *tinajón*, he will fall madly in love with her and never leave Camagüey.

Camagüey City

The city of Camagüey (population 275,000) was founded in 1514 by Velásquez along the banks of Nuevitas Bay, on the northern coast. Originally called *Santa María del Puerto del Príncipe*, the settlement was considered vulnerable to attack and shifted to the banks of the Río Caonao in 1516. A group of disgruntled Indians razed that settlement to the ground resulting in another transfer inland to its present site 16 years later. The city's long-winded name was then abbreviated to *Puerto Príncipe*, before it was again shed in favour of Camagüey.

In spite of its new location, the town was repeatedly sacked by pirates, including the notorious Englishman Henry Morgan who torched it in 1668. The town was later rebuilt in a maze pattern (to confuse looting marauders), and eventually grew in importance to play a leading role in the country's struggle for independence.

Today the city's meandering streets, with their sharp turns and abrupt dead-ends - plum places for an ambush - and the sober, deferential buildings that line them, lend the city a distinctive colonial flavour.

How to get there

By Air

There are three flights weekly from Havana for $52 (one way).

By Train

Trains run daily from Havana for $22. The railway station is on Ave Carlos J Finlay, north of the city.

Accommodation

Villa Maraguan, Camino de Guanabaquilla, Circunvalante Norte, ph 72160 - 50 rooms, pick of the city's hotels, both hotel and bungalow-style accommodation, very pleasant, nightclub, pool - $30-37.

Camagüey, Carretera Central Km 41, ph 82 490 - 142 rooms, out of town, Soviet-style architecture, good food, pokey atmosphere, pool - $29-35.

Plaza, Calle Van Horne 1, ph 82 413 - 68 rooms, central location, comfortable, good rooms and facilities - $29-34.

Puerto Príncipe, Ave de los Mártires y Andres Sancjez, La Vigia, ph 7575 - 79 rooms, nothing out of the ordinary - $25-31.

Gran, Calle Maceo No 67 e/ Ignacio Agramonte y Gral, Gómez, ph 2093 - 72 rooms, central location - $25-31.

Eating Out

Parador de los Tres Reyes, Plaza San Juan Dios - very reasonable Cuban and Spanish food.

Meson La Campaña de Toldeo, Plaza San Juan Dios - more of the same.

Coppelia, Parque Ignacio Agramonte.

Sightseeing

The best and easiest way to navigate the city's sights is by foot. A good place to start is the **Parque Ignacio Agramonte**, on Calle Martí. During colonial times the square was the site of parade grounds, and in later

KEY TO MAP

•	ACCOMMODATION
1	Motel Las Cuevas
13	Costa Sur
14	Ancón
•	EATING
11	Colonial Trinidad Restaurant
12	Guamuhaya Restaurant
•	OTHER
2	La Canchánchara
3	Museo de la Lucha Contra Bandidos
4	Parque Martí
5	Iglesia de la Santísima Trinidad
6	Museo Municipal de História
7	Museo de Arqueologea
8	Galeria de Arte Universal
9	Museo de Arquitectura Colonial
10	Casa de la Trova

TRINIDAD CITY

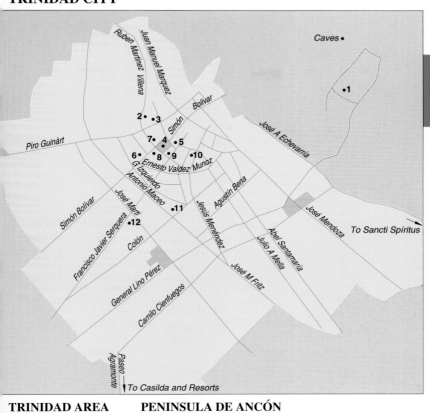

Caves •

•1

Ruben Martinez Villena

Juan Manuel Marquez

Bolívar

Simón

2 • •3

José A Echevarría

Piro Guinàrt

7 • 4 • 5

6 • 8 • 9 •10

G. Izquierdo

Ernesto Valdez Muñoz

Antonio Maceo

Agustín Bena

•11

Simón Bolívar

José Martí

Jesús Menéndez

Jose Mendoza

To Sancti Spíritus

Abel Santamaría

Julio A Mella

Francisco Javier Serquera

•12

Colón

General Lino Pérez

José M Fritz

Camilo Cientuegos

Paseo Agramonte

↓ To Casilda and Resorts

TRINIDAD AREA

PENINSULA DE ANCÓN

Trinidad

Casilda

ninsula de Ancón

Location Map

•13

•14

CAMAGÜEY

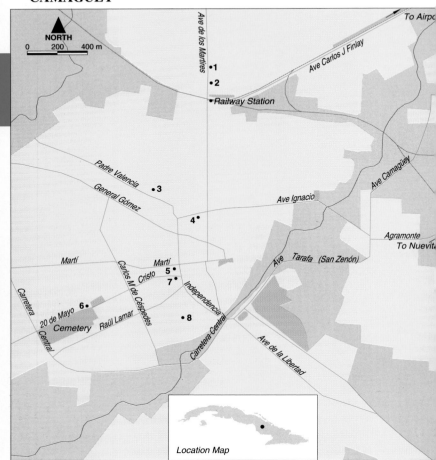

Accommodation
1 Puerto Príncipe
4 Gran

Other
2 Museo Provincial Ignacio Agramonte
3 Teatro Principal
5 Parque Ignacio Agramonte
6 Iglesia de Santo Cristo del Buen Viaje
7 Catedral
8 Plaza San Juan de Dios

years, the scene of a number of executions of Cuban independence fighters including Andrés Manuel Sánchez. In memory of these martyred heroes, it is now wreathed at each corner by palm trees. Dominating the square is a statue of General Ignacio Agramonte (1841-73), the city's most famous son who was a general of Camagüey's rebel forces during the Ten Years War. His birthplace, the **Casa Natal de Ignacio Agramonte**, lies three blocks north at Calle Agramonte No 59 - count the number of *tinajones* in the courtyard and see how up-to-date the family was.

Immediately south of Parque Ignacio Agramonte is the lofty city **Catedral**. A 10-minute walk past the cathedral, along Calle Cisnero, is the charming **Plaza San Juan de Dios**, surrounded by colourful single-storey dwellings. Built in the 18th century, the square was recently listed as a national monument.

The **Teatro Principal**, built in the mid-19th century, is north of the square on Calle Padre Valencia. This solid marble building hosts local spectaculars - a mixture of dance and operatic recitals - and is the home of the excellent Camagüey Ballet. The last northward stop, just beyond the railway station, is the large and very impressive **Museo Provincial Ignacio Agramonte** (1848). Formerly a garrison for Spanish soldiers, then a grand hotel, it's now a museum with exhibits of period furniture and local archaeological discoveries.

Attractions west of the square are few and far between but the **Iglesia de Santo Cristo del Buen Viaje** (1844), a small church along Calle Cristo, is worth a visit. Behind the church is the attractive city cemetery.

Santa Lucía

A pleasant two-hour drive east of Camagüey City, near the important port of Nuevitas, is the popular beach resort of Santa Lucía. From afar it looks just like any other stretch of Cuban sand, with lots of cheesy thatched-roofed cabanas only a stone's throw from the sea. But a closer inspection reveals an area alive with possibilities - offshore is a trove of spectacular dive sites that would rank as some of the best on the island. The warm, translucent waters are ideal for diving among over 50 species of coral (including rare black coral), marine crustaceans and an infinity of fish, including prowling sharks. For many, though, the highlight is visiting two sunken wrecks, the *Mortera* and the *Pizzaro*, both of which went down in the late 19th century.

Hotels, usually filled with orthodontically corrected Canadians and Europeans, organise horseback rides, pleasure cruises and fishing trips. Most tourists refrain from such activity, preferring to sip cold glasses of *Tínima* (the local beer) at the beach bars instead.

Accommodation

Villa Coral, Playa Santa Lucía, Nuevitas, ph 48 236 - 338 rooms, bungalow-style accommodation on beach, good services, hires underwater equipment and arranges diving classes, car rental, disco, pool - $40-48.

Villa Caracol, Playa Santa Lucía, Nuevitas, ph 48 302 - 160 rooms, two-storey bungalow-style accommodation, also hires underwater equipment, child-care facilities, nightclub, pool - $40-45.

Mayanaho, Playa Santa Lucía, Nuevitas, ph 48 184 - 237 rooms, balconied rooms facing ocean, landscaped garden, quiet, pool - $35-40.

Detail at base of Statue of Antonio Macco.

EASTERN CUBA

The country's five easternmost provinces are where most come seeking *'el sabor de Cuba'* - the flavour of Cuba. With their emphatic mix of race and culture, beach and mountain, rum and tobacco, and heat - lots of it - satisfaction is easily guaranteed.

The region begins with **Las Tunas**, which has few attractions apart from a pleasant northern beach, then extends across to **Holguín**, scene of an intimate moment in the country's history - a seasick, travel-weary Columbus first came, saw and was conquered by his obsession with gold here. Inland is the history-making province of **Granma**, dominated by the slopes of the Sierra Maestra mountains, and Bayamo, a city with an evocative and rebellious past. **Santiago de Cuba**, the island's second largest city and the 'cradle of the Revolution', is further to the south. Throughout its history the city has witnessed the arrival of settlers from France and the Caribbean area - Carnival time, with trumpeters, drummers and dancers by the score, is an obvious time to visit. At Cuba's easternmost corner is the little-visited province of **Guantánamo**. Attention here is focused on two completely different attractions: the charming colonial city of Baracoa; and the Guantánamo Naval Base, site of past and present unease.

The region also boasts **Guardalavaca**, lagging only behind Havana and Varadero as the island's most popular resort, good walks and a wealth of archaeological sites.

Las Tunas Province

Noted today for nothing in particular, save the production of sugar and chemicals, Las Tunas Province is remembered as the scene of a fanciful story of religious devotion. In 1510, the shipwrecked Spanish sailor Alonso de Ojeda embarked on a long and perilous journey across the land, carrying little bar a statue of the Virgin Mary which he had salvaged from the boat. Along the way he pledged to present the statue to the first village he happened to stumble upon. True to his word, when he arrived at Cueyba he gave the image to a startled Indian chief with the instructions that he was to start building a church. The site of this church was propitious - it was apparently the first place where the Catholic faith was acculturated in Cuba.

Over 300 years passed before the province set up government and in 1853, Las Tunas (the name means 'prickly pears') was finally decreed a city. Razed by rebel troops in 1897, the city was desultorily rebuilt, and is today remarkable for its total lack of character. Attractions outside of Las Tunas City are just as scarce but **Playa Covarrubias**, a 4km strip of silky white sands on the northern coast, is a picturesque diving and swimming spot with a good lookout.

How to get there

By Air
Flights from Havana are $57 (one way).

By Rail
Trains run daily from Havana for $26.

Accommodation
Las Tunas, cnr Ave 2 de Deciembre and Carlos J Finlay, ph 45 169 - 154 rooms, Soviet-style architecture, nightclub, pool - $25-33.

Holguín Province

The fourth largest province in Cuba and the third most populous, Holguín was originally the home of the *Taíno*, an advanced Indian population who arrived in the country in the 12th century. It was also the place, in 1492, where Columbus first set foot on Cuban soil. Enamoured by the region's beauty and convinced of its potential deposits of gold, Columbus hung around long enough to appreciate the former, but, after exploring the southern coast on a second voyage, forlornly dismiss the latter.

Gold may not have been forthcoming but nickel certainly was - it now accounts for 15% of Cuba's export revenue. Most of the nickel mines and processing plants are in Moa, Nicaroa and Punta Gorda. Sugar, tobacco, citrus fruits, heavy machinery and fishing make up the bulk of the province's other main industries.

The landscape is variegated with mountain ranges, rolling countryside dotted with citrus orchards and sugar plantations, lush valleys, and one of the most visited beaches on the island.

Holguín City

The provincial capital, Holguín City (population 200,000) was founded in 1525 by Captain García Holguín but it wasn't declared a municipality until 1752. For years a sleepy country town, it has since developed into a thriving, industrial city. Most sights are easily walked, especially around the main square, but a taxi or car is required to reach the city's principal lookouts.

How to get there

By Air

There are four flights weekly from Havana for $60 (one way). The Frank País International Airport is south-west of the city.

By Rail

Trains run every other day from Havana.

Accommodation

Pernik, Ave Jorge Dimitrov y XX Aniversario, ph 48 1011 - 208 rooms, apparently named after the birthplace of Bulgarian leader Georgi Dimitrov, reasonably handy location, lumpen decor, enormous lobby, tennis court, pool - $33-41.

El Bosque, Ave Jorge Dimitrov, ph 48 1012 - 72 rooms, nightclub, pool - $22-27.

Villa Cayo Saetia, Carretera a Felton, Mayarí, ph 42 5350 - 15 rooms, bungalow-style accommodation, quiet and peaceful, good food and facilities - $22-25.

Mirador de Mayabe, Alturas de Mayabe, ph 48 2160 - 24 rooms, out of town, small and friendly, pool - $20-24.

Sightseeing

The city's busy centre is the **Parque Calixto García**, between calles Frexes and Martí, which is named after a Holguín native and general in the wars of independence. Around the park is a complex system of back alleys, where you can still find areas of traditional colonial architecture - small houses with spacious courtyards, artisans' galleries, cafés and the like.

North of the square, at Calle Frexes No 198, is the **Museo Provincial**. The museum is housed in a building memorably known as *La Periquera* ('Parrot Cage'), coined after Spanish soldiers - bivouacked here behind barred windows, dressed in colourful uniforms and set upon by rebel troops during the Ten Years War - took on the appearance of caged birds. Inside are displays on local history and a number of Indian artefacts including the famous Holguín axe, a rock sculpture of a man that was discovered in the mid-19th century.

South of the square, on Calle Maceo between calles Martí and Luz Caballero, is the **Museo de Historia Natural**. There is an interesting collection of ornithological exhibits as well as a room containing brilliantly painted *polymita* shells (from tree-dwelling snails endemic to the eastern provinces). Further along Calle Maceo is another square, the **Parque de San Isidoro**, dominated by a large statue of Karl Marx, with the beautiful **Iglesia de San Isidoro** (1720) just to the south.

In the city's outskirts, passed unfinished buildings and peeling one-storey houses, lies the **Plaza de la Revolución**. Surrounded by tall umbrageous trees, the square holds a mausoleum made from marble which is the final resting place of Calixto García.

West of Holguín is the popular **Loma de la Cruz**. Over 400 steps lead up the hill to a lookout with great views over the city, while a cross, erected at the top in 1790, is the site of an annual local pilgrimage. Another good vantage point is the **Mayabe Lookout**, a short drive south of the city. There's more good views - this time overlooking Mayabe Valley - plenty of tourist facilities, and if it's not nursing a hangover in the shade, *Pancho the Ass*, a bleary-eyed, beer-guzzling burro.

About 30km north of the city is the coastal village of **Gibara** (also known as Villa Blanca). It's a pleasant enough town but the real drawcard in the area is the offshore island of **Cayo Saetia** (45 sq km). This remote spot has a series of cove-shaped beaches that are perfect for swimming and snorkelling. The island is also home to an abundance of fauna including antelope, buffalo and deer. Nearby is the haloed **Puerto Bariary**, the place where Columbus first landed in Cuba on 28 October 1492.

Guardalavaca

One of Cuba's most popular and fastest-growing resorts, Guardalavaca is 57km north-east of Holguín City. Its name is an abbreviation of *Guardalavaca y Guardalabarca* ('Guard the cow and Guard the ship') and harks back to the days when the locals unlawfully traded with smugglers, hiding contraband cattle aboard the ships whenever the authorities were making their rounds.

Today most travellers come for the standard diet of white-sand beaches and diaphanous blue seas, good seafood and 10km of dive sites which include Boca de Esponjas, el Canon de los Aguajies and El Salto. The *Eagle Ray Diving Centre* can rent boats, snorkelling and scuba diving equipment. Hotels and tourist agencies can also arrange jeep seafaris and helicopter tours.

Accommodation

Rio de Luna, Estero Ciego, ph 30 202 - 230 rooms, very private, good facilities, car rental, pool - $40-48.

Atlántico, Playa Guardalavaca, ph 30 280 - 365 rooms, newish, on the beach, comfortable rooms, exterior and interior walls lined with mosaics and murals, good gym, child-care facilities, extensive daily activities, pony rides, live Cuban music, very popular, pool - $40-45.

Guardalavaca, Playa Guardalavaca, ph 30 145 - 261 rooms, bungalow-style accommodation, lots of recreational activities, gym, car rental, close to dive sites, large pool - $40-45.

Don Lino, Playa Blanca, ph 20 443 - 145 rooms, cheap alternative, private bath, nightclub, pool - $20-25.

Chorro de Maita and Banes

Just a few kilometres east of Guardalavaca is **Chorro de Maita**, the largest Indian burial site in Cuba. Over one hundred skeletons - most in mint condition - have been unearthed including those of farmers, craftspeople, women and children luxuriating in precious jewellery, and curiously enough, even the bones of a Spanish *conquistador*. The site was discovered in 1978 and recently declared a national treasure.

Further south-east is the nondescript town of Banes, the birthplace of former Cuban dictator Fulgencio Batista (the rumour mill here suggests he was once a cane cutter for Castro's father). Only one real attraction exists but its a good'un - the unique **Museo Indocubano**. This museum contains a wealth of archaeological debris found in the province, mostly from the Chorro de Maita site. Among the exhibits are skeletons, ceramics, pottery, tools, jewellery, and a teensy-weensy gold figurine, thought to date from the 13th century. The museum is at Calle General Marrero No 305. Opening times are Tuesday to Saturday from 9am-5pm and Sunday from 9am-1pm. Admission is $1.

NOTES

Granma Province

Granma is a province of contrasting topography: the imposing peaks of the Sierra Maestra in the east; and the flat plains of the Río Cauto, which muddily snakes some 250km through the area, in the west. Steeped in a history of contraband trade and bold insurrection, Granma Province is today a quiet backwater, dependent upon an economy of sugar and coffee. It was given its present name when Cuba was divided into 14 provinces in 1976 - fittingly after the queerly named boat which bought Castro and his comrades to the province's south-western shores.

Bayamo

Bayamo (population 125,000) is the provincial capital and the second township founded by Velázquez in Cuba in 1513. Formerly known as San Salvador de Bayamo, it was originally the site of a large Indian population. The town prospered on the back of sugar, coffee and cattle, and its location near the waterways of the Río Cauto meant it was soon a major transit point for smugglers and black-market racketeers.

But what makes Bayamo such an exception is its history of rebellion. In 1604, the Bishop of Cuba, Fray Juan de las Cabezas Altamirano, was kidnapped in Bayamo by the French pirate Gilbert Giron. Incensed by his demands - which included an extortionate ransom - the townspeople overran Giron's hide-out and cut off his head. The slaying inspired what is reputedly the first poem written on Cuban soil, the *Espejo de Paciencia* (Mirror of Patience).

On 10 October 1868 the wealthy landowner and fanatical chess player Carlos Manuel de Céspedes issued the *Grito de Yaya*, a proclamation of independence and a call to arms. He subsequently freed the slaves at his sugar plantation and led a revolutionary force of 147 men against the Spanish, determined to wrest Bayamo from their control. Ten days later he succeeded. (The *Bayamo Anthem* was penned at this time, which became the national anthem.) Soon after, in 1869, the rebels burned the city to the ground, rather than surrender it to the re-gathered Spanish troops. Céspedes was named 'Father of the Country' in recognition of his efforts but was slain in San Lorenzo while protecting his bishop (he was playing chess, remember?) in 1874.

Almost a century later, in 1953, a poorly equipped rebel force attempted to storm an army garrison in Bayamo. Planned to coincide with Castro's attack on the Moncada barracks in Santiago de Cuba, the ambush provoked a similar disaster - most of the men were machine-gunned to death within the first ten minutes.

Since the Revolution, there's been little call to inspire the city's renowned rebel spirit. Bayamo has simply kept on keeping on, a semi-industrial city unobtrusively making its way by producing rice, sugar, beef and dairy products.

How to get there

By Air
Flights from Havana are $60 (one way).

By Rail
Trains run daily from Havana for $27. The railway station is east of the city.

By Road
Bayamo is 842km from Havana. Roads link the city from Las Tunas, Holguin and Santiago de Cuba.

Accommodation

Sierra Maestra, Carretera Central a Santiago de Cuba, ph 48 1013 - 210 rooms, good location close to the city centre, comfortable, reasonable food, pool - $35-41.

Sightseeing

The **Plaza de la Revolución**, along Calle General García, is the city's hub and the best place to begin a tour of the city's sights. Here you'll find a statue of Céspedes and a bust of 'Perucho Figueredo', who composed the Bayamo Anthem. Legend has it that Figueredo was asked to write the anthem in order to stir local patriotism. But he had to do it quickly. Upon being told, Figuerdo promptly climbed off his horse, pulled out a piece of paper and wrote the verses using his saddle as support.

Overlooking the Plaza de la Revolución to the south is the **Poder Popular** (the city government). This is where Céspedes, as the voluntarist President of the Republic of Cuba, declared the end of slavery in Cuba. His birthplace is a lovely 18th-century mansion on Calle Maceo, just north of the square. Now the **Museo Carlos Manuel de Céspedes**, it has rooms furnished with the many trappings (a chess set no less) and accomplishments of his life. The **Museo Provincial**, documenting the city's fight for independence, is next door.

To the west of the square is the **Plaza del Himno**, meeting place of the locals after the city was captured by Céspedes troops in 1868. This is also the spot where they gathered to sing the national anthem. Nearby is the beautiful **Templo del Santisima Savador de Bayamo** (1516), one of the country's oldest churches, which surprisingly survived the 1869 fire. It has since been declared a national monument.

Manzanillo

The province's second largest city and its main port, Manzanillo (population 100,000) lies west of Bayamo on the Gulf of Guacanayabo. Its dowdiness is enlivened only by the Moorish flavour of its architecture and the knowledge that it is the birthplace of the popular musical form, *son*. Just outside the city is **La Demajagua**, the sugar plantation once owned by Céspedes. His house has now been turned into a museum with the bell he used to gather his slaves still hanging for all to see.

Accommodation
Guacanayabo, Ave Camilo Cienfuegos, ph 54 012 - 120 rooms, slow service, pool - $20-25.

Media Luna and Playa Las Coloradas

Fifty km south of Manzanillo, along the coastal highway, is Media Luna ('Half Moon') where Celia Sánchez was born on 9 May 1920. Sánchez was Castro's long-time factotum: fellow-revolutionary, admirer, cook, nurse, secretary and lover. She died from cancer in 1980 and was buried with full military honours. Her home is now a museum.

Further south along the coastline is the narrow, swampy Playa Las Coloradas, the place where Castro and his men landed from the *Granma* on 2 December 1956. Within moments of their arrival they were spotted by Batista's plants and sicked by government troops. Soon the castaways were either captured, wounded or killed. Little has been erected to mark that momentous event apart from a commemorative pathway symbolically leading in the direction of the Sierra Maesta, and a large, weed-clogged square.

The Great Sierra Maestra National Park

These mountain ranges, stretching the length of Granma province, have played a prominent part in shaping Cuba's turbulent modern history - Castro and his rebels hid out here from Batista's troops between 1956-9 before they rode in triumph through Havana. Since then they have become a geographical term for revolutionary nirvana, much like Sherwood Forest was to Robin Hood.

Now Cuba's largest national park, the area supports an excellent range of wildlife including the *tocororo*, nightingale, woodpecker and the rare *jutias* (Cuban possum). The park is also rich in plant life and features a number of good walks, with the Morlote-Fusete and El Guafe trails the most popular.

Musician in Havana.

Accommodation

Villa Turistica Santo Domingo, Santo Domingo, Bartoleme Maso - 20 rooms, cabin-style accommodation, arranges excursions into the Sierra Maestra, close to good walks, pool - $20-23.

Tours

Hotels and tourist agencies in Bayamo and Manzanillo can arrange day tours to the Sierra Maestra National Park. The Villa Turistica Santo Domingo also provides similar services. One of Cuba's true wilderness areas, it is accessible only by car.

Santiago de Cuba Province

The second most populous province in Cuba, Santiago de Cuba is dominated by the Sierra Maestra range in the south and vast sugarcane plains to the north. Pico Turquino (1972 metres), in the lower fringes of the Sierra Maestra, is Cuba's highest point.

The province is one of Cuba's most important producers of sugar, tobacco, coffee and citrus fruits, as well as copper. In recent years it has experienced considerable industrial development, especially the city of Santiago de Cuba, thanks to Soviet money and its favourable spot on a deep harbour. Unfortunately, Cuba can no longer rely on its former benefactor, which means the plants, mills and factories now sit idle or half-built.

Santiago de Cuba City

One of the most visited destinations in the country, Santiago de Cuba City (population 1,100,000) was founded by Velázquez in 1515 at the entrance of the Río Paradas and then moved a year later to its current location. Formerly the official residence of the Spanish colonial governors, it was, for a short while, the country's capital, until that honour was bestowed upon Havana in 1553.

For the early settlers, gold was the most sought after commodity. While their prospecting proved futile, it did lead to another discovery - vast deposits of copper. Thereafter the region was known as *El Cobre*, with the first copper mine opening in 1547.

Subsequently sacked by pirates in the early part of the 17th century, the most notorious being Jacques de Sores, the city set about constructing an elaborate system of fortifications. The defences proved of no avail, however, and were blown to smithereens by Henry

Morgan and his raiding party in 1662.

In 1791, large groups of French settlers poured into the city, fleeing the slave uprising that had paralysed Haiti. They brought with them advanced coffee and sugar-growing techniques, and their skills - coupled with an influx of African slaves - meant the city soon prospered.

Since then Santiago de Cuba has played an important historical role in the country's independence. The mulatto Antonio Maceo, a general in the Ten Years War and one of the leaders of the second war of independence, was raised here. Castro too spent much of his time in the city. He returned, in 1953, to lead the ill-fated attack on the Moncada barracks. The coup was a bloody mess: the attackers, mostly students with little or no military training, either got lost on the way or were massacred at the scene. Castro and his brother Raúl escaped to the city's outskirts but were apprehended a couple of days later. Their skins were saved only after the intervention of the city's archbishop (a friend of Castro's father) and a fortuitous mix-up - rather than being sent to the army barracks and certain death, the Castro brothers were locked up in the local gaol.

In 1984, the city was conferred the 'Hero City of the Republic of Cuba' in honour of its revolutionary past.

Today Santiago de Cuba is the second largest city in Cuba - a noisy, jostling provincial capital, swarming with people at all hours. With its fusion of races and their flourishing traditions, the city is also known as the 'Caribbean Capital of Cuba'.

One-way streets, peso hotels and cramped, dusky houses dominate the colonial centre while on the outskirts there are wide tree-lined avenues, high-rise apartments, an excellent university and the city's best range of accommodation.

How to get there

By Air

There are two daily flights from Havana for $65 (one way). An overnight tour from Havana (including return airfare) is $159. The Antonio Maceo International Airport is 8km south of the city.

By Rail

Trains run three times weekly from Havana for $35 and take around 17 hours (give or take the odd delay). The railway station is on Ave Jesús Menéndez, a short walk west of the city centre. A Ferrotur sign hangs drolly outside an old building across the railway tracks; skip it, the real office is on the first floor.

Tracks of my Fears

The whistle blew; the train started up and pulled slowly out of Havana's central station. It was 4.59pm, exactly on time. In just under 17 hours I would be in Santiago de Cuba.

Or so I thought.

Several hours into the journey, the train stopped. The lights popped on in the cabin. A conductor with a hairpiece like a pan scourer was moving through the train - a kilometre trip from end to end - informing passengers that heavy rains had washed out the track a little further on. He talked very quickly as if he was terrified he was going to be interrupted. Nobody in the cabin said a thing. Buses had been arranged to pick us up, he said, and take us to the next station, beyond the waterlogged track, where another train was waiting to take us to Santiago de Cuba. He paused. 'But there is a problem,' he continued. 'There is no petrol to put in the buses'.

The conductor vanished in the ensuing uproar.

We waited. And we waited some more. We waited through the heat and we waited through the boredom. After twenty-four hours of waiting for *those* buses they finally arrived. (Some passengers - clearly nettled by all of this - had done the sensible thing and upped and left in the night; they were last seen traipsing through fields, a suitcase in each hand.)

Everybody trooped wearily off the train, then waited a few more hours to be loaded onto the buses. It took another hour before we reached the station but by that stage no one was counting - after all, who cared as long as we were moving. Early the next day, the train pulled into Santiago de Cuba. It had been almost two days since we'd left Havana.

I got off, dishevelled but delighted to turn my back on the damned train.

By Road

Santiago de Cuba City is 876km from Havana. The Autopista Nacional leads directly into the centre.

Tourist Information

There is a tourist office at Calle Rene Carbo No 5; the staff can provide information on the Carnival as well as arrange tours throughout the city and surrounding attractions such as La Gran Piedra (see under the heading **Parque Baconao** later). The Banco Financiero International is at Calle Aramades No 565.

A post office is at Calle Aguilera No 517 and you can make international calls from an office in the Catedral foundations. There is a Photoservice branch at Calle Félix Pena No 552 and another on Calle Victoriano Garzón, just south of the Las Américas Hotel.

Accommodation

Santiago de Cuba, Ave de las Américas y Calle M, ph 42 612 - 322 rooms, one of the best hotels in Cuba, Canadian-designed, all mod cons, great views of the city from the tops storeys, good shops and friendly service, live Cuban music, tennis court, lovely Hockney-blue pool - $69-83.

Villa Gaviota, Ave Manduley 502 e/ 19 y 21, ph 41368 - 53 rooms, located in the posh neighbourhood of Vista Alegre, close to La Maison store, good facilities, pool - $28-37.

Las Américas, Ave de las Américas y General Cebreco, ph 42 011 - 68 rooms, excellent alternative to the Santiago de Cuba Hotel across the road, comfortable rooms, bike hire, nightclub, pool - $26-35.

Balcón del Caribe, Carretera del Morro, ph 91 011 - 96 rooms, close to Castillo del Morro, good views overlooking sea, quiet, popular nightclub, pool - $25-34.

Villa San Juan, Carretera Siboney y Parque San Juan, ph 42 434 - 64 rooms, historical location (Spain and the USA signed the city's surrender in 1898 under a ceiba tree in the grounds), some distance from the city, villa-style accommodation, pool - $24-29.

Universatario MES, Calle L y 7, Rpto Terrazas, ph 42 398 - just north of the Las Américas Hotel and spitting distance from the university, the city's cheapie, shared bathroom, large, plain rooms, good food, very friendly - $15-19.

Excellent rooms in the city centre can be rented from Rodolfo Massipe, Calle San Carlos No 57, ph 27 457 for $10-15 a day.

Local Transport

Car

Cars can be rented from the Santiago de Cuba and Las Américas hotels.

Taxi

There are taxi stands outside the main hotels. A taxi from the Santiago de Cuba Hotel to the city centre is $4; double that if you want to go to the airport.

Eating Out

Apisun, Calle San Pedro y Heredia - good location near Parque Céspedes, light snacks, quiet, very friendly staff, great place to sip *canchánchara*.

Café Las Isabelica, cnr calles Aguilera and Calvario - good range of coffees, light snacks, always busy.

Casa del Te, cnr calles Aguilera and Enremada - tea house serving light snacks, good value.

Coppelia, Calle Victoriano Garzón.

El Barturro, cnr calles Aguilera and Hartmann - Spanish cuisine.

El Morro, Castillo del Morro - Cuban and Spanish food, brackish coffee, spectacular views, pricey.

Matamoros, cnr calles Aguilera and Calvario (across the street from Cafe Las Isabelica) - expensive though delicious Spanish cuisine, lots of excellent live entertainment, the pick of the city's restaurants, very popular.

1900, Calle San Basilio e/ Pio Rosada y Hartmann - steak, turkey and rabbit dishes, elegant dining.

There are plenty of *paladares* in the city including one at the friendly home of Raúl Quintana, 5ta Rita No 97 e/ Carlos Dubois y Callejoa.

Entertainment

Kung fu and action movies are the all the rage at the *Cine Rialto*, on Calle Félix Pena (opposite the Catedral). For live music, try any one of the larger hotels or the *Bacardí Bar*, 500 metres north of the railway station on Ave Jesús Menéndez. The excellent *Casa de la Trova*, Calle Heredia No 206-8, is the best venue in the country for the indigenous ballad form *'nueva trova'*. Performances by local and visiting troubadours are extremely popular so get there early if you want a seat. Tapes and CDs, soft drinks and alcohol are sold inside. Admission is free.

The *Tropicana Santiago*, also known as the 'Nightclub of the Caribbean', features the same gala shows, grand costumes and has the same expensive drinks as its lustier Havana rival. You'll have to take a taxi to get there as its north-east of the Santiago de Cuba Hotel, on the city's outskirts.

The *Santiago Carnival*, the most famous in Cuba, is again celebrated after being postponed or reduced since 1991. And when its on, as it was in late July 1995, the city goes off - costumed revellers dancing, drinking and eating until dawn; brightly lit decorations; and everywhere the sound of drums and cornets.

SANTIAGO DE CUBA CITY

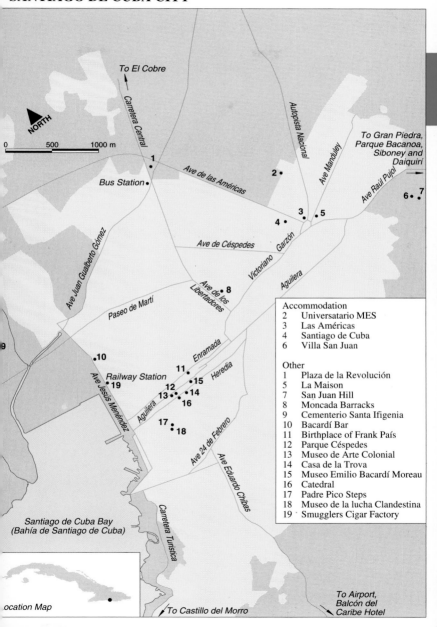

To El Cobre

Carretera Central

NORTH

0   500   1000 m

1   Plaza de la Revolución

Bus Station

Ave de las Américas

Autopista Nacional

Ave Mandulley

To Gran Piedra, Parque Bacanoa, Siboney and Daiquirí

Ave Raúl Pujol

2   Universatario MES

6 • • 7

3 • • 5

4 •

Ave de Céspedes

Victoriano Garzón

Aguilera

Ave Juan Gualberto Gómez

Ave de los Libertadores

• 8

Paseo de Martí

Enramada

• 10

Railway Station

• 19

11

12   • 15

13 • • 14

16

Heredia

Aguilera

Ave Jesús Menéndez

17 • • 18

Ave 24 de Febrero

Ave Eduardo Chibas

Santiago de Cuba Bay
(Bahía de Santiago de Cuba)

Carretera Turística

Location Map

To Castillo del Morro

To Airport, Balcón del Caribe Hotel

Accommodation
2   Universatario MES
3   Las Américas
4   Santiago de Cuba
6   Villa San Juan

Other
1   Plaza de la Revolución
5   La Maison
7   San Juan Hill
8   Moncada Barracks
9   Cementerio Santa Ifigenia
10   Bacardí Bar
11   Birthplace of Frank País
12   Parque Céspedes
13   Museo de Arte Colonial
14   Casa de la Trova
15   Museo Emilio Bacardí Moreau
16   Catedral
17   Padre Pico Steps
18   Museo de la lucha Clandestina
19   Smugglers Cigar Factory

For something a little less frenetic, you can while away the afternoon playing chess on a first floor patio on the corner of calles Félix Pena and Heredia.

The New Cuban Song

Although 'Neuva' Trova had been in evidence in Cuba since the 1960s it wasn't until a decade later, with the work of its three main interpreters - Silvio Rodríguez, Pablo Milanés and Noel Nicola - that the song form gained national prominence. Much of their inspiration was drawn from the Beatles, and especially the albums *Revolver* and the hallucinatory *Sgt Pepper's Lonely Hearts Club Band*, which stimulated new possibilities for song lyrics. No less influential were the US civil rights movement, the Vietnam War, and the popularity of Bob Dylan, Joan Baez and Peter Seeger as protest singers. Back at home 'Nueva' Trova found probably its truest ally in a revolutionary culture which demanded a politically conscious and literate artist.

Today the 'new' Cuban song has a vast and adoring public ever eager to listen to the music - and, more importantly, the words.

Shopping

Apart from hotel shops, a few dollar stores on calles Enramada and Aguilera, and a handicraft parlour at Calle Félix Pena No 675, there's only the exquisitely expensive La Maison left. Housed in an old mansion in the up-market Vista Alegre neighbourhood (near the Santiago de Cuba Hotel), this department store has a range of fashions, jewellery and perfume every bit as good as that on offer at its namesake in Havana. An al fresco café in the grounds serves snacks, coffee and alcohol - the ideal place to put your feet up and count the remainder of your dough.

Sightseeing

Parque Céspedes, in the heart of the city, is the gathering place for *santiagueros* (be prepared for the usual buffeting - 'Hey mister! Where you from!, etc') and a good reference point to begin a walking tour. On the east side of the square is the **Casagranda Hotel**, formerly the city's premier lodgings (at the time of writing it was closed for renovation), while to the south is the pink **Catedral** (1522), which contains a small museum on local church history. To the north is the **Ayuntamiento**, where a triumphant Castro first stood, staring down the crowds, following the Revolution. He still occasionally goes into rhetorical overdrive here but the building is usually reserved for the municipal authorities.

Nearby, on Calle Felix Pena, is another place of interest - the **Museo de Arte Colonial**. Built in the early 16th century, it is supposedly the oldest existing mansion in Cuba. Diego Velázquez is thought to have lived on the top floor; he apparently used the ground floor for smelting gold which was then shipped back to Spain. Since then the buildings been a hotel, Masonic Lodge, clerical offices and now a museum crammed with antique furnishings, mostly lifted from the city's colonial nobiliary. Admission is free.

Running contiguous with Parque Céspedes is Calle Heredia. Here you'll find the **Casa de la Trova,** a library across the road displaying photographs of historic city landmarks, and the home of José María Heredia, an eminent 19th-century poet. The street is closed to vehicles on weekends, when it becomes the focus of a giant outdoor party for the locals.

A block north of Calle Heredia is the **Museo Emilio Bacardí Moreau** (1899), Cuba's second oldest museum. Unfortunately it was closed for renovation at the time of writing. The **Museo de Carnaval**, which features exhibits commemorating the city's many festivals, is a few blocks south, as is the old Jesuit **Colegio Dolores** (literally the 'school of pains') where Castro was taught.

West, along Calle Diego Palacios, is the **Museo de la Lucha Clandestina**. Formerly the city's police station, it was attacked by Frank País - second in command to Castro and leader of the urban arm of the M-26-7 Movement - in 1956. The assault was a diversionary tactic as Castro was just off the coast and about to land aboard the *Granma*. País survived but was ambushed and killed by police two years later. The museum has a number of good exhibits telling the story of País and the rebel fight against the government. **Padre Pico**, the city's famous steeped street and a popular neighbourhood hang-out, is immediately below.

Further west towards the bay, then right on Ave Jesús Menéndez, is the railway station and, across the street in a small, inauspicious building, a smugglers' cigar factory. You're more than welcome to come inside, browse around and watch the *torcedores* (cigar rollers) at work. Most of these cigars are destined for Havana where they're sold to tourists as the real thing (they aren't). Continuing north, on the same side, is the rum factory built by the Bacardí family. Inside is a shop that sells a range of cheap rum and Ché T-shirts. It's also a venue for live music at night.

Much of the city's remaining sights are flung further afield and are better reached by car or taxi.

North-west of the city, off Ave Crombet, is the **Cementerio Santa Ifigenia** (1868). This impressive cemetery is the burial place of national luminaries such as Céspedes, Palma and José Martí, who rests in a huge mausoleum, surrounded by the shields of the Latin American republics, and cloaked in the Cuban flag. A number of other revolutionary heroes are also exhibited for veneration.

The **Moncada Barracks**, on Calle Carlos Aponte, is the city's principal attraction. These buildings were stormed on 26 July 1953 by a revolutionary force headed by Castro (he drove the leading car, apparently without his glasses which he detested wearing in public). Castro had chosen as his target the second largest garrison in Cuba - a curious choice when you consider only 134 terrified, ill-equipped rebels were facing off against a thousand well-armed troops. In his favour was the Carnival, celebrated the opposite of Havana in the middle of summer, which he thought would distract the attention of the soldiers stationed at the barracks. In the event it didn't matter as the attack was bungled from the start. Castro, because of the dim light or because he wasn't wearing glasses, pranged his car in the barracks compound. Disturbed by the commotion, a soldier approached the car and was immediately shot - the element of surprise was therefore lost. Pretty soon, the night was filled with the crack of rifle fire and the brat-a-tat-tat of machine guns. After the smoke had cleared, all the leaders were dead apart from Castro (one of the men later recalled that he had felt like a 'Carib kamikaze'). Those that were wounded were either rounded up or finished off. Later, the surviving raiders, including the Castro brothers, were pardoned by Batista. By then Castro had begun plans for another insurrection.

Part of the compound now houses a school and the **26th of July Historical Museum** documenting the events of that night. Bullet holes are still visible on many of the walls. Admission is $1.

Further east, along Calle Victoriano Garzo, then left along Ave de las Américas, is the distinctive 15-storey **Santiago de Cuba Hotel** (the city's best hotel), the **Universidad de Oriente** (which has Spanish-language courses for foreigners), and the **Plaza de la Revolución**. The square, a showpiece for the 1991 Pan-American Games, features an enormous bronze statue of Antonio Maceo that makes your chewing gum cleave to the roof of your mouth.

Sport and Recreation

There is a large baseball stadium on Ave de las Américas. Matches are usually played on a Friday or Saturday night during the season (November-June). Admission is one peso.

Outlying Attractions

Castillo del Morro

About 8km south of the city, along the Carretera Turistica which hugs the shoreline of Santiago Harbour, is the Castillo del Morro. Originally constructed in 1633, the fort was destroyed by the unscrupulous English pirate Henry Morgan in 1622, rebuilt in the 18th century, then refurbished and reopened in 1978. It was designed by the Italian engineer Juan Bautista Antonelli, the man responsible for the del Morro and la Punta forts in Havana. Inside is a labyrinthine network of passages and rooms, some with iron stocks used for shackling prisoners, still in place. The views from the ridges of fortification are stunning. There's also the **Museo de la Pirateria**, which has corny exhibits tracing past pirates (roll on up Jacques de Sores and Henry Morgan!) to present-day plunderers (well, hello the CIA!). Its all a bit rum really (I half expected to come across a room called Ye Davey's Locker).

Cayo Granma

This small island lies at the entrance of Santiago de Cuba Harbour. It was originally called Cayo Smith after its owner, who proceeded to turn the island into a resort for foreign holidaymakers. Little trace remains of its former status and it now has a distinctly laid-back, Cuban feel to it. The island's not blessed with a surplus of sights but it does have a good bar and restaurant. There is no accommodation on the island.

Cayo Granma can be reached by daily ferry from Ciudadmar, on the Carretera Turistica.

El Cobre

The scruffy town of El Cobre (named after the opening of the first copper mine in the Americas) is 16km north-west of the city. There's not much of interest here apart from a church rising above the town which is revered as the sanctuary of the **Virgen del Cobre** (or the 'Sanctuary of Our Lady of Charity'). According to legend, three devoutly religious fishermen set out in their boat when they were caught in a great storm. Just as they thought they were about to drown, they came across a statue of the Virgin Mary floating in the swells. They scooped the figure up and, convinced that its heavenly powers would rescue them, made their way safely back to shore.

Over the years, the statue - now safely enclosed behind a glass case - has been visited by thousands of worshippers and in 1916, was named the patron saint of Cuba. For many though, the real highlight is the huge collection of propitiatory offerings that have found their way to the church. Included among them are baseball gloves, T-shirts, plaques placed by Soviet construction workers, Hemingway's 1954 Nobel Prize for Literature gold medal, and a little golden figure presented by Castro's mother - perhaps asking safe passage for her sons.

Dos Ríos

Immediately north of El Cobre is the town of Dos Ríos. It was here, on 19 May 1895, that José Martí was killed in an obscure skirmish. His death was both shattering and inexplicable: a bad horseman and an even worse shot, Martí broke command and rode off in the direction of a Spanish column. Shot in the neck, he lost balance and fell from his mount. A scout of the Spaniards then approached the fallen figure, lifted his revolver and despatched Martí to martyrdom.

Only months into the second campaign for independence, Martí lay dead. He was a national poet, freedom fighter, hero, saint, epochal achiever and reasonably good looking - made to order for popular idolatry. A monument marks the spot where he fell.

Parque Baconao

Along Ave Raúl Pujol, which runs east from a roundabout near the Las Américas Hotel, is **San Juan Hill**, the final battlefield of the 'Spanish-American War'! A large ceiba tree marks the spot where the Spanish surrendered to US forces on 16 July 1898. Further east, along the same road - which is dotted with billboards and monuments commemorating those who died in the Moncada attack - is Parque Baconao (800 sq km). Declared a Biosphere Reserve by UNESCO, it is another of Cuba's gigantic recreational parks, stretching from the outskirts of the city to Laguna Baconao and nestled between the Sierra Maestra cordillera and the waters of the Caribbean. Within its boundaries are historical sites, rock formations, gardens, coffee plantations, an incongruous theme park and several beaches.

About 12km east of Santiago de Cuba is the **Granjita Siboney**. This farmhouse, rented by Abel Santamaría, was the headquarters of Castro and his men prior to the storming of the Moncada barracks. (Santamaría, who helped conceive the assault, was killed soon after.) Now a museum, it displays clothing (Carnival-type outfits, a few fatigues, etc), weapons, personal possessions and newspaper accounts of the events of that night. Admission is $1. Six km past here is Siboney, a popular weekend beach for Cubans but nothing out of the ordinary.

Further east is the **El Valle Prehistoric**. This theme park, a monument to Cuban kitsch, contains 243 life-size ferroconcrete dinosaurs - the biggest being a 27-metre-long Diplodocus. What the park's doing here is anybody's guess but families with young children will find it a lot of fun. Admission is $1.

A pretty drive 18 km east of the city, along a steep road that leads into the sierra, is the **La Gran Piedra** ('Giant Boulder'). And big it certainly is, weighing 75,000 tonnes and standing almost 1300 metres high. The crag is believed to be the remains of an ancient volcano that was worn away by erosion. From the summit you can apparently see Haiti and Jamaica on a clear day; I couldn't (and it was crystal clear) but the views are nonetheless spectacular. Nearby is the **Jardines de la Siberia**, an extensive botanical garden with a good variety of native plants, and the **Museo La Isabelica**, a former coffee plantation.

Parque Baconaos other attractions, all within short reach, include a car museum, the resort town of *Daiquirí* (no connection to the cocktail) and the location of a good swimming and snorkelling beach, and Laguna Baconao, an up-and-coming tourist complex.

Accommodation

Bucanero, Parque Baconao, ph 7126 - 200 rooms, bungalows fashioned from river boulders, on the beach, pool - $25-30.

Balneario del Sol, Parque Baconao - 125 rooms, more polished boulders, pool - $25-30.

Villa Daiquirí, Parque Baconao, ph 24 849 - 157 rooms, on the beach, lots of water sports available, very friendly, pool - $22-26.

Villa La Gran Piedra, Parque Baconao, ph 5224 - 44 rooms, hotel and bungalow-style accommodation, great location high up in the hills, close to the La Gran Piedra rock, quiet - $25-34.

Guantánamo Province

Languishing at the easternmost tip of Cuba, Guantánamo is a mountainous, sparsely populated region streaked by many rivers including the Miel and the Yumurí. A distinctive feature of the landscape is the abundance of *molitongos* (large, quaintly shaped boulders), which are found in the south.

Guantánamo was a former centre of the peaceful *Taíno*. Their disposition soon changed with the arrival of the Indian chief Hatuey, who warned them of an impending invasion from nearby Hispanola. In 1512, Velázquez and his landing party came ashore and were soon met with tremendous resistance. For two months, Hatuey and his small band of men - transformed almost overnight into stealthy hit-and-run guerillas - pinned the Spanish down. But Hatuey's days were numbered; he was captured soon after and burned at the stake. The Indians fared little better. Brutal treatment, warfare, disease and poor nutrition quickly decimated their ranks.

As the native population declined, African slaves filled the gap, working the province's thriving sugar and coffee plantations. But since the heydays of the 18th and 19th centuries, the province has largely stuttered along, and it is now one of the poorest regions in Cuba. Sugar and coffee are still produced but it is salt that provides most of the economic sustenance. Even the construction of *La Farola* ('The Beacon') in 1959, an overland road linking Baracoa to the rest of the island, hasn't eased matters. Adding to its woes is the colonial spectre of the US-controlled Guantánamo Naval Base, once so important to the local economy but now cut off.

The Guantánamo Naval Base

The Guantánamo Naval Base houses some 7000 Americans - servicemen and their dependents - who live amid all the comforts of a typical US town. Personnel can visit the shopping mall, the radio station, the bakery, the dentist, whatever they fancy. About two dozen Cubans work in the base, which is otherwise out of bounds to the rest of the island and the world at large.

The base's inception in 1898 ostensibly stemmed from the desire by the USA to shore up its political, economic and military influence in the Caribbean. To that end, the Americans convinced Cuba to accept the Platt Amendment, written as an appendix to the Cuban Constitution of 1901, which in part protected the new base. In the same way Cuba was convinced to sign two further treaties on Guantánamo in 1903 and 1934. The pretext for all of this was to maintain Cuba's independence, and as a security measure in accordance with the interests of the USA.

Since 1903, the USA has had an indefinite lease; the annual rent is $4085. The Americans promptly send a cheque which is duly left uncashed by the Cuban government who, since the Revolution, have viewed its existence as a continued act of colonisation. The naval base is also seen as a violation of international law, since according to the treaties it was leased, not sold, to the USA as a coaling station and for other naval purposes. However, only mutual agreement between the two countries or US abandonment of the area can terminate the lease.

The Guantánamo Naval Base (continued)

The base effectively shut up shop in 1959 when Castro came to power. It has since undergone extensive fortification, largely to deter the increasing numbers of Cubans seeking asylum. Its popularity as a refuge has even inspired a joke:

Q. 'Whats Cuba's national anthem? A. 'Row, row, row your boat...

But for some it is no laughing matter. There are currently over 30,000 refugees (both Cuban and Haitian) housed in the base, most living in tents or hastily constructed sheds, awaiting their fate. Long-term confinement has meant some have resorted to slashing themselves with wire or drinking bleach in the hope of being flown to the USA for medical treatment.

Those that tired of waiting returned home by braving minefields, scaling barbed wire or even swimming, regardless of the shark-infested waters

For President Clinton, there are few options but to continue with his present policies. If he brings the Guantánamo refugees to the USA, he risks alienating voting Americans who are opposed to further immigration. A decision to allow the refugees entry would almost certainly spark another Cuban exodus, much like an eerie replay of the Mariel boatlift in 1980. In addition, Clinton is tied to an agreement he made with Castro in 1994 to grant over 20,000 exit visas each year to Cubans who want to leave - visas issued not from Guantánamo but from Havana.

Yet keeping the status quo may not be good enough. Even though families with children are now allowed to leave the naval base and enter the USA (under the provisions of a special parole program), the rest of the refugees will continue to remain.

Guantánamo City

Apart from a decrepit main square, a quaint 'zoo where all the animals are made of stone', the city's proximity to the naval base, and the fact that most of Cuba's salt is produced here, there is little to recommend.

South-east of the city is **Caimanera**, a coastal fishing village just a short swim away from the base. Again, there's little in the way of tourist attractions here but the atmosphere - with its uniformed guards, Checkpoint Charlies and restricted areas - is positively film noir. A short drive away is a tangle of Cuban sentry towers and wire fences, and on the horizon, the Guantánamo Naval Base.

How to get there

By Air

Flights from Havana are $73 (one way).

Accommodation

Caimanera, Loma Norte, ph 99 414 - 26 rooms, newish, good food, views of the base, friendly service - $25-33.

Guantánamo, Calle 13 Norte e/ Ahogado y 1 Oeste, ph 36 015 - 142 rooms, Soviet-style architecture, gloomy atmosphere, reasonable food, arranges tours to see naval base - $22-27.

Tours

Day tours to a lookout above the base can be arranged with hotels and tourist offices in Santiago de Cuba and Guantánamo cities. The view from the top is haunting - beneath you is no man's land, like the former border between East and West Germany, jammed with machine guns, one of the largest minefields in the world, electric traps - all triggered by electronic devices - and finally, at the mouth of the bay, the naval base. Turn the shirt collar up and say to yourself, 'This is me in Guantánamo'.

Tours should be booked well in advance.

Baracoa

Cuba's easternmost city, Baracoa was founded by Velázquez in 1512 on the banks of the Río Maniguanigua. It was the island's earliest settlement, and for a brief while Cuba's first capital (1512-15), until that honour was conferred on Santiago de Cuba. From here, the conquest of the rest of the country began.

For centuries settlers, merchants and curious travellers could only reach the mountain-locked city by sea, but the building of a highway now allows easy - and spectacular - access.

Today it is an unspoiled, captivating city of narrow cobble-stone streets and tile-roofed houses. Tourism is big business in Baracoa and this, coupled with the production of coffee and cocoa, provides the bulk of the city's income.

How to get there

By Air

Flights from Havana are $79 (one way). An overnight tour from Havana (including return airfare) is $159.

By Road

Baracoa is 1069km from Havana, 150km from Santiago de Cuba City and 98km from Guantánamo City. From Guantánamo City, a picturesque road heads along the southern coastline where it links with La Farola. This major highway then winds through 30km of precipitous vegetation before dropping steeply down to the bay at the entrance of the city.

Accommodation

Porto Santo, Carretera al aeropuerto, ph 43 512 - 87 rooms, car rental, arranges rafting tours down a nearby river, pool - $34-42.

El Castillo, Calixto García, Loma del Paraíso, ph 42 103 - 34 rooms, housed in an old fort, good views over the city, above average food, friendly, pool - $33-42.

Eating Out

La Punta - north west of the city, good setting in an old fort, mainly Cuban food, unexceptional.

Sightseeing

At the entrance of the city, overlooking the bay, is the **Fuerte Matachín** (1739-42). One of three fortifications built by the Spanish to protect the city from pirates, it's now a museum highlighting the achievements of the region. Further west is the charming **Parque Central**, the gathering place for the local faithful. A statue of the redoubtable Indian chief Hatuey stands in the centre. East of the square is the **Iglesia de la Asunción**, a church thought to have been built soon after the town's founding. Inside is what is regarded as the oldest symbol of Christianity in the New World - *La Cruz de la Parra* ('The Cross of Vine') - allegedly the cross planted by Columbus when he first arrived in 1492. Made of wood, the cross seems to have shrunk over the years (one of the likely explanations is that it has been whittled down by eager-beaver believers wanting a souvenir).

Baracoa's other highlight is the **Malecón**, a seawall almost as long - and just as popular with the locals - as the promenade in Havana.

West of the city is the table-topped mountain known as **Yunque de Baracoa** (*yunque* means anvil). Formerly the site of a large Indian population and later a refuge for escaped slaves, it's now said to be used by local sailors as a guide when approaching the harbour.

INDEX

LIST OF MAPS